CREATING COMMUNITY ACCEPTANCE FOR HANDICAPPED PEOPLE

CREATING COMMUNITY ACCEPTANCE FOR HANDICAPPED PEOPLE

By

ROBERTA NELSON

CHARLES C THOMAS • PUBLISHER
Springfield • Illinois • U.S.A.

Published and Distributed Throughout the World by

CHARLES C THOMAS • PUBLISHER
Bannerstone House
301-327 East Lawrence Avenue, Springfield, Illinois, U.S.A.

ISBN 0-398-03788-4

Library of Congress Catalog Card Number: 78-3615

With THOMAS BOOKS *careful attention is given to all details of manufacturing and design. It is the Publisher's desire to present books that are satisfactory as to their physical qualities and artistic possibilities and appropriate for their particular use.* THOMAS BOOKS *will be true to those laws of quality that assure a good name and good will.*

Original manuscript draft funded by a grant from McDonalds Corporation.

Printed in the United States of America
V-R-2

Library of Congress of Congress in Publication Data

Nelson, Roberta, 1936-
Creating community acceptance for handicapped people.

Bibliography: p. 207
Includes index.
1. Handicapped. 2. Social Integration.
3. Fund raising. I. Title. [DNLM: 1. Handicapped.
2. Rehabilitation. 3. Attitude to health.
HD7255 N429c]
HV3000.N44 362.4 78-3615
ISBN 0-398-03788-4

In Thanksgiving
for
Carol, Craig, and Robert

PREFACE

THE first half of the rehabilitation process is educating, training, and helping disabled persons and their families to function as fully as possible in all areas of life.

The second half of the rehabilitation process is eliminating the handicapping conditions within the community.

This book is devoted to presenting an integrated though limited body of knowledge which is aimed at "treating the community" or teaching the community to be supportive and accepting of people with differences.

Voluntary fund raising can and should be used as a tool in the social action process of integration. Negative attitudes are changed through education and involvement.

The mechanism available to motivate people to become involved in being supportive and accepting of handicapped people is circular — the needs of handicapped people are met through satisfying the self-fulfillment and ego needs of normal people by providing them with the opportunity to help handicapped people. The roles of giver and recipient are interchangeable. The benefit is mutual.

ACKNOWLEDGMENTS

THIS book was written to share the experience and observations of 12 years of community organization and another 6 years spent in helping to develop a comprehensive system of services for handicapped people in an urban county from 1970 to 1976. The philosophical and financial support generated helped to create needed services and an environment of acceptance for people with more than ordinary problems.

The results of the 6 year experience in developing the community to be more responsive were gained with the help of hundreds of individuals. Some, however, are not quoted in the text but deserve special recognition for sharing their knowledge, talent, time and resources. Outstanding professional colleagues were Robert Vogt and Bill Kelsay, now both in HEW, Dr. Jeri Kelsay, now with the Illinois Office of Education, T. K. Taylor of the Joint Commission for Accreditation of Facilities for the Developmentally Disabled, Dennis Popp, Developmental Disabilities coordinator in Kansas, P. J. Trevethan, the late internationally known rehabilitation pioneer, John Wojtowicz, Director of Residential Services at Ray Graham and Jim De Ore, Executive Director of Ray Graham, Dr. Dominic Parisi, Director of the Administration Studies Center at De Paul University, and Don Moss of the Illinois Association for Retarded Citizens.

Since most of the achievements of the community development program were the result of voluntary contributions of time, talent and resources of volunteers, I must name those who were most outstanding. Dorothy Unger and Marilyn Morrison, both parents of children with limitations and both volunteers extraordinaire. Joining them in giving time and sheer hard work were Ruth Nevaril, Lee Micko of Michel Kazan, Madeline

Spradlin, Pat Nerad, Jill Garrett, Mary Perina, and Trilby Porter. Iona Glos and her family Gordon and Ginevra Bednorz, Paul Butler, Mary Meyers, Anna Hanson, Brooks McCormick, Hank and Alben Bates, Jay and Rollie Dunteman significantly and unstintingly shared their financial resources. Dave Gooder, the brilliant and creative partner in the law firm of Lord, Bissel & Brooks, John Cartland, partner with Arthur Andersen, and Joe Abel, Planner for DuPage County gave freely of their specialized talents and knowledge.

To fellow overachievers Vickie Schklair, Margaret Pfrommer, Phyllis Stearner, Barbara Bechdol, Rami Rabi, Bill Scaman and Augie Christman who don't let mental retardation, quadriplegia, paraplegia, cerebral palsy, blindness, epilepsy, or armlessness stand in their way I acknowledge my source of continued inspiration to hang in there when things get really tough.

And finally, a book does not get written without the aid of long suffering secretaries and typists, and this one was done over a 3 year period with the help of Marcia Logan, Arlene Lambert, Marcia Rohr, with the final draft for publishing by the world's most impeccable typist, Opal Dietelhoff.

The concepts and experiences in this volume represent one approach, one set of observations. The goals of community acceptance are achievable in a multitude of ways, I'm sure, but this is a place to begin understanding how to create positive change.

CONTENTS

Section IV. The Issues in Rehabilitation and Habilitation

Section V. Fund Raising and Support Organizations

Section VI. Summary

CREATING COMMUNITY ACCEPTANCE FOR HANDICAPPED PEOPLE

SECTION I
The Problem and How to Change It

Chapter 1

THE PROBLEM

A RECENT nationwide Gallup poll sponsored by the President's Committee on Mental Retardation (PCMR) revealed that only 9 percent of the people interviewed would object to six mildly or moderately retarded persons who have been trained for community life occupying a home on their block.[1] PCMR noted that the poll presented results of what people say they would do or believe. "Their statements may not always be reflected in their subsequent actions."

The governor of Michigan received an award from the PCMR for starting a new program of twenty-three such group homes for retarded people in Michigan.

At the same time, the city council of a small town in Michigan, having just become aware of several such group homes in its community, faced a stormy group of citizens who objected to living near retarded people and voted the group homes out of existence, saying they did not meeting zoning requirements. Two weeks later a recommendation was made to build an institution for mentally retarded citizens next to the hospital sometime in the future.

In a midwestern city, homeowners in a middle-class neighborhood brought suit against the city council for granting a special use permit to a not-for-profit organization to rent apartments and provide training in daily living skills for mentally retarded people.

A month later in a small, middle-class, midwestern community angry neighbors called their homeowners' association president to protest having five mentally retarded and physically handicapped children, ages five through twelve, move into a house with houseparents in their attractive suburban

[1]The Gallup Organization, *Public Attitudes Regarding MR* (Princeton, New Jersey, December 3, 1974).

neighborhood.

In another upper-middle-class, suburban neighborhood, homeowners called their alderman, had a meeting, and criticized the seller of two small apartment houses for permitting the new owners to buy the buildings and rent apartments to mentally retarded young women. In the first case, the home was closed; in the second case, the suit was judged in favor of the group home; in the third and fourth cases, the projects went ahead.

These occurrences of rejection observed by the author because of proximity were repeated a hundredfold throughout the country as small groups of retarded people moved into the community. In each case not *everyone* in the neighborhood was opposed to having retarded people live near them, but the dissenters were far more vocal than the assenters or neutral parties.

The introduction of people who were substantially different into the neighborhood represented a change which threatened a number of persons' sense of security.

The people answering the Gallup poll were being truthful, but they were reacting to an academic question rather than facing a real situation. It is obvious from our own experience that as the degree of remoteness of the integration of disabled people into the mainstream of community life decreases, anxiety increases. It is philosophical acceptance versus real acceptance. The Judeo-Christian ethic which controls the basic value system in the United States dictates the obvious "right" answer to the question in the poll, "No, I wouldn't mind having six mentally retarded people live in a group home in my block." Yet, all across the country, organizations trying to start group homes and other residential alternatives confront situations similar to the above cases. What accounts for the difference in acceptance?

Is it the difference between having what we wish and reality? To construct another academic choice, which three of the following would you most like to have for yourself and your loved ones?

1. A physical disability

2. Good health
3. Mental retardation
4. A high degree of intelligence
5. Poverty
6. Enough resources to live comfortably
7. A jail sentence
8. Someone who cares for you
9. Drug addiction, mental illness, alcoholism
10. The ability to cope with life

Two, four, six, eight, and ten will receive more votes because they are generally acceptable, desirable traits. They are real but they represent the good things in life. One, three, five, seven, and nine are equally real but they are not popular or desirable. The pain that is experienced by having to face and deal with the odd numbered choices can lead to personal strength and achievements that might never be available to our even numbered winners. That pain, however, also causes breakdown and flight or defeat. The people who have odd numbered problems are many, but those traits are still considered stigmatizing and undesirable.

William Gellman[2] maintains that after the evolution of rehabilitation from a healing art to an applied discipline with two decades of growth and expansion, rehabilitation entered a new stage which combines the development of treatment theory with advocacy and "service to the individual with the creation of an open community in which the disabled and disadvantaged can use their abilities proudly and productively."

Through community action Kandel[3] believes that rehabilitation may itself be viewed as tertiary prevention.

Kurt Lewin's[4] dictum that behavior is a function of the person interacting with the environment, indicates that society itself may be perpetuating and encouraging handicapped behavior on the part of the disabled person.

---

[2]W. Gellman, *Rehabilitation Practices with the Physically Disabled* (Columbia Union Press, 1973).

[3]D. Kandel and R. Williams, *Psychiatric Rehabilitation: Some Problems in Research* (New York, Atherton Press, 1964).

[4]K. Lewin, *Principles of Topological Psychology* (New York, McGraw-Hill, 1966).

Gellman says, "The existence of such impediments to the rehabilitants' effective performances necessitates intervention in social and community situations to change attitudes and behavior of significant individuals in the rehabilitants' life space." Volumes have been written regarding the technology of changing the disabled person to an able person. Similarly, significant resources are available regarding counseling the family of the rehabilitant; but a substantial void is present regarding the changes required in the general community.

This book proposes to first identify the barriers to the acceptance of deinstitutionalized handicapped people and those already living in the community; then to discuss the underlying concepts for creating social change; and finally to recommend the outline of a social action plan for achieving integration of disabled people.

This book is intended for all individuals, professionals and laymen alike, who have an interest in improving the quality of life for disabled people by enabling them to live, work, and play side by side with the nondisabled in the community.

Chapter 2

WHY IS INTEGRATION NOT OCCURRING — IDENTIFYING THE BARRIERS

IN order to create change, we must first identify the restraining forces which are inhibiting change.

The first half of the rehabilitation process is educating, training, and helping the disabled person to function as fully as possible in all major life areas. In teaching the disabled person to cope, those people who provide his immediate environment, his family and even close acquaintances, are involved in the process of helping him to function. Gellman[1] says, "Many individuals are handicapped because society's attitudes turn the biases of the nondisabled into handicaps for the disabled." The nondisabled person's bias that disabled people cannot function competently is the handicapping condition which keeps the disabled person from living and functioning fully.

The second half of the rehabilitation process must then be education and training the community to accept people with differences and encourage them to live in the mainstream of life. Many obstacles still exist which prevent disabled people from living freely and fully. Just as there are barriers which prohibit disabled people from functioning in the community, so are there barriers which prevent the nondisabled from accepting the disabled as people with responsibilities and the right to live in the least restrictive environment possible.

An obvious barrier to the functioning of disabled people in the community is the presence of a large institution designed as a residence for disabled people. This distorts the proportion of handicapped people in a given small community, and tends to

[1]W. Gellman, *Rehabilitation Practices with the Physically Disabled* (Columbia Union Press, 1973).

isolate the institutional population rather than integrate them into the mainstream of society. This insulated existence intensifies the degree of handicap of each individual because it limits opportunities for interaction with normal people and, therefore, puts a lid on the opportunity to learn normally acceptable behavior. At the same time, the community may have a strong economic interest in the presence of the institution and will vigorously oppose its reduction or elimination.

Institutions were started in the eighteenth and nineteenth centuries as a humane way to provide for the "feeble minded and insane" and to protect the community from presumed danger. Dorothea Dix,[2] the famous social reformer, sought to persuade legislators and other influential citizens with both humanitarian and economic appeals, "It is cheaper to take charge of the insane in a curative institution than to support them elsewhere for life." Recent research indicates that institutions do not always best meet the needs of either mentally retarded or mentally ill people. Dr. Henry Cobb notes that the massive growth of the institutionalized population occurred in the twentieth century rising steadily as a proportion of the total population until 1967. (See Scheerenberger's report.) Wolfensberger,[3] the most outspoken recent intellectual advocate for normalization, recommended deinstitutionalization and a normalized life style for mentally retarded people. He proposed that a variety of residential alternatives with varying degrees of supervision would enhance the opportunity for each person's development.

However, the institutions which arose to meet the needs of mentally ill and mentally retarded people are still frequently the main industry in small towns. To close them down now means putting thousands of people out of work. Therefore, the superstructure of institutions remains, even though community programs are also developed. The cost per capita for institutional care is now frequently far higher than for community

---

[2]R. H. Bremner, *American Philanthropy* (Chicago, University of Chicago Press, 1960), p. 69.

[3]R. B. Kygel and W. Wolfensberger (Eds.), *Changing Patterns in Residential Services for the Mentally Retarded* (Washington, D.C., President's Committee on Mental Retardation, 1969).

care. The rationale for maintaining both institutional and community programs is that community programs prevent people from future institutionalization but institutions must still be maintained because community services are not yet in existence.

One of the primary barriers to the development of community services is lack of funds. In 1978-79, the Illinois state operated facility budget for developmentally disabled people is $162,000,000 to serve 6,500 residents. The state budget for community based programs is $52,000,000 to serve approximately 448,000 developmentally disabled people in need of service. Thus, the monies needed to operate community programs are limited because so many dollars are committed for institutional care. This has been reinforced by the lure of federal dollars through qualification of institutions as "intermediate care facilities (ICF/MR)" under Title XIX of the Social Security Act.

Three Major Barriers to Deinstitutionalization

The largest single barrier to deinstitutionalization is the pressure of vested interests in operating institutional "residential" programs. The needs of the mentally retarded, the mentally ill, and the physically handicapped have been subjugated to the needs of the people employed in these institutions. To permit a large number of currently institutionalized disabled people to move back to their own community with appropriate support services would result in unemployment in the town where the institution is located or depopulation of nursing homes. This barrier is difficult to overcome. Legislators for the districts in which institutions are located fight to maintain the institution because their constituencies want to keep their jobs and the legislators say, "If those guys lose their jobs, I lose their votes." The cost is high, not only in tax dollars but also in terms of opportunities lost to the mentally retarded people who must remain dependent in order to protect employment opportunities for the nondisabled.[4] Yet closing the institutions means

[4]United States Department of Health, Education & Welfare, *Mental Retardation Source Book of the Department of HEW* (Washington, D.C., Office of MR Coordination). →

high unemployment and the creation of another social problem. Either the state must provide tax incentives to attract other industries to these communities and start other public programs in those communities, or mental retardation will continue as the main industry and deinstitutionalization will never become a reality. The state employee unions must be called upon to help solve the problem with the understanding that their primary concern is not the needs of disabled people; it is jobs for their members.

The second barrier to deinstitutionalization is lack of day programs and residential alternatives in all communities. A system of comprehensive day-care support services must be available in the community before a diversified residential program can succeed, and the funding must be available to provide the community service delivery system.

The third barrier to deinstitutionalization is the expressed preference of families of disabled people to keep their disabled child who already lives in an institution, there. Once the family has made the decision to institutionalize their child or other family member, it creates discomfort for them to consider other alternatives. The decision to institutionalize a family member is frequently an agonizing one. To reopen the problem of "what's best for John" is to reopen pain. In addition, families and parents see that the state has a greater likelihood of always being there than a community not-for-profit agency. Therefore, the state-operated facility is perceived as a safer, more stable environment than the community services being proposed for their disabled member.

The Barriers to Integration

The first barrier to integration into the community by disabled people are the 75 to 500 bed shelter-care homes and warehouses operated by for-profit entrepreneurs. When deinstitutionalization first began in the 1960s, many retarded,

---

In public institutions for mentally retarded persons:
In 1963 there were 197,516 patients and 69,494 employees.
In 1967 there were 193,188 patients and 94,900 employees.
In 1971 there were 181,009 patients and 118,909 employees.

mentally ill, and physically handicapped residents of state institutions were moved into something euphemistically called community "progams."

The communities in which these programs were located were not involved in planning or implementing the migration of residents from the state hospitals to community "warehouses" or institutions. Private for-profit entrepreneurs bought up old hotels and nursing homes and announced to the Department of Mental Health, "Our program has '100 beds', '200 beds', '400 beds'." The legislature and administration saw cheaper dollar signs on an annual care basis and rushed to legislate the funds for "community care." The cheaper dollar signs have resulted in hundreds of thousands of people receiving minimal food and shelter with no developmental programming. Is it really more economical to move someone from a state hospital where per capita costs were $9,000 a year to a for-profit care facility at a per capita cost of $6,000 a year if a planned program of developmental activities is not part of the care? The lack of developmental programming keeps the disabled person dependent and forecasts a lifetime in that facility at a cost of $240,000 (40 years x $6,000 a year). In many instances nursing care for a severely physically handicapped person may be $12,000 to $18,000 a year in a nursing home.

A good residential program with an intensive developmental component might cost $9,000 a year, but after a period of time the mildly and moderately retarded person has a high likelihood of becoming substantially self-sufficient. Given appropriate rehabilitation support services and architecturally modified housing, the physically handicapped individual can live at significantly less cost to taxpayers and in many instances become self-sufficient.

The for-profit organizational goal by its very nature is often in conflict with the goals of habilitation or rehabilitation. The bottom line for a profit oriented business must be "how much financial benefit is returned to the owner." The bottom line of habilitation or rehabilitation programs is how many people improved their functioning ability, in what measurable increments, and finally how many have moved into less restrictive environments and how many have found employment.

A factory owner could not make a profit if he repeatedly and deliberately asked his best and most productive workers to leave and in fact helped them find jobs elsewhere, while keeping all his less productive workers. Yet that is what a rehabilitation workshop must do to be effective. Its end goal is human profit-productive workers, not financial profit.

Similarly, a for-profit residential program cannot make money unless they operate with an economy of scale involving 75 to 400 beds. This many disabled people in one residence without adequate staffing and environmental facilities makes it just as much a human "warehouse" as the traditional custodial institution and automatically insulates the residents from integration into the community. To have 400 substantially different people in one building is to automatically put the neighbors on the defensive. Even in a densely populated urban area, the normal minority of developmentally disabled people (2 percent) can become a threatening majority of perhaps 50 percent, if 400 disabled people live in one facility in one block. People may tolerate the presence of this group but will perceive them as interlopers, thus there is no normal interaction — no one offers to give the disabled person a ride to church, no one brings him a loaf of bread, there is no chatting neighbor-to-neighbor when mowing the lawn, raking leaves, or walking down the street. Only the small living unit which maintains a normal population balance permits this kind of interaction.

In carrying the profit motive one step further as a barrier to integration, the entrepreneur operates profitably by keeping beds filled and thereby maximizes potential income. Unless he has a waiting list to fill the beds, his motivation to move people out to more independent residential programs is not high. A cash bonus to the operator for each person moved out might result in moving people out before they are ready, thus increasing the chance for failure. The result can be permanently damaging to the disabled person's confidence that he can indeed succeed.

For-profit enterprises have created a strong economic system in the United States. However, there are some activities which are best conducted where the organizational goal is measured in human terms rather than monetary terms. Some experts in human services feel it is doubtful that full servicing in the community can be accomplished without proprietary facilities of a variety of kinds. The inclusion of proprietary facilities requires standards for operation and judicious use of public subsidies.

It would seem imperative that the purpose of the organization and its goals must be in concert with the goals of rehabilitation, habilitation, and integration if the process of providing opportunities for disabled people to develop and live independently is to succeed.

Second Barrier to Integration — Architectural Barriers

Physically disabled people are prevented from integrating into the community because architectural barriers impair their ability to move from place to place. Architectural barriers prevent the people with limited mobility from gaining access to buildings, parks, and housing — a high curb is difficult to navigate in a wheelchair, a flight of stairs is impossible. Such barriers may keep a person with a mobility problem a prisoner in his own home.

Third Barrier — Lack of Public Transportation

The lack of access to public transportation, the lack of public transportation systems, and the lack of specialized transportation services keeps many disabled people socially isolated and unable to seek employment.

Fourth Barrier — Negative Attitudes of People in the Helping Professions

Once they have physical access to the community, disabled people face the less visible but very real obstacle presented by the negative attitudes of most people.

The negative attitudes found in the general public are also

found among individuals who work in the helping professions. The Harasymiw, Horne, and Lewis studies[5] indicate that professionals view disabled people as inferior in the same way as the general public (see Chapter 8). The inability to function in a major life area is intensified if the very people who are helping improve the disabled person's ability have the ultimate expectation that the person being helped cannot really function equally with the normal person.

Fifth Barrier — Negative Attitudes of the General Public

The emotional reaction of many people which generate and perpetuate negative attitudes toward disabled people are devasting obstacles to integration. The result of these reactions prevents many handicapped children from attending school, playing and living with normal children, and prevents handicapped adults from living in the community. Lack of understanding by neighbors frequently puts pressure on the parents of the handicapped adult, especially males, to "put him away with his own kind." Parents, not wishing to have their child experience any more rejections, will many times comply with their neighbors' wishes. The crime of removing a disabled adult to a more restrictive environment because of ignorance on the part of the general public is a crime against both the disabled individual and society as a whole. The crime against the individual is precisely that. He has been deprived of his rights as a citizen accorded him by the United States Constitution when he is not permitted to live as a free person in the mainstream of life. The only justification for removal of a citizen from the mainstream of life should be that his presence in a nonrestrictive environment constitutes a danger to himself or society. This may be true for some severely emotionally disturbed people or the habitual criminal. It is clearly not true of all disabled people.

The doctor who tells a parent "your child has epilepsy, give

---

[5]S. J. Harasymiw, M. D. Horne, and S. C. Lewis, *Attitude Congruence of Handicapped and Non-Handicapped Towards Disability Groups,* Paper presented at National Rehabilitation Association National Conference, Cincinnati, Ohio, October 15, 1975.

him his medicine and just don't tell anyone" creates the opportunity for a seriously damaged self image and gives advice which in fact perpetuates negative attitudes. The epileptic feels, "If what I have is so terrible I can't tell anyone, there must be something really bad about me." It is not too surprising to find the incidence of epilepsy much higher among prison inmates. The 25 percent unemployment rate of people with epilepsy reflects the prejudice which drives people to behave in socially unacceptable ways against the society that rejects them.

The crime against society is the perpetuation of a system that eliminates or, at the very least, inhibits the productivity of an individual. In fact, a restrictive environment turns a human being into a dependent person, simultaneously using large quantities of tax dollars to maintain that dependent "tax burden" status and forcing the rest of society to pay the bill.

Gunnar Dybwad[6] states, "As much as possible, normalization implies maximizing a retarded person's community participation. Obviously, there are degrees of integration, depending upon the severity of the handicap. Maximal integration is achieved by the retarded person who lives in an ordinary family setting in ordinary community housing, who moves and communicates typically for his age, limited though he may be, and who utilizes, in typical ways, typical community resources such as schools, churches, hospitals and clinics, bowling alleys, swimming pools, and job placements. For others, this pattern of maximal integration is not feasible; they are in need of one or more specialized services within a restrictive environment. The important, and too frequently neglected, point is that this should be considered transitional. The individual should constantly experience opportunities for developmental growth which might lead to a more normalized environment."

Most learning is by imitation. Therefore, the disabled person has the greatest opportunity to develop to an optimal level and learn normal behavior when he is integrated with normal models. However, a community which rejects the disabled person cannot be a model to emulate.

---

[6]G. Dybwad, Symposium on residential care, p. 83.

Whether negative attitudes are of aversion, repulsion, fear, guilt, anger, or pity, there is a need to remove these attitudes from the minds of the general public in order to gain broader acceptance of people with differences. Over the years and cross-culturally, attitudes toward disabled people have varied from reverence to fear and aversion. To understand how to change negative attitudes, we must remember that this attitude of normal man toward disabled man has a long history.

Dr. Cobb maintains, "Public attitudes are not static, but old attitudes may persist as sub-surface layers which make people's behavior variable and inconsistent as they are subject to different pressures, by no means universal, however."

Von Hagen states, "The Mayans and most primitive cultures believed there was no such thing as chance or accident; what we call accident was to them purposeful. It revealed that evil influences were at work even before the 'accident' and that the intended victim had been selected; it was a sign of malignant influences. We acknowledge 'accident'; they thought about the supersensuous realities of the incident."[7]

Von Hagen in referring to the Incas tells us that even though affliction, referring to physical deformity, was felt to be a punishment from God, primitive cultures often tried to improve the state of the afflicted.

According to Gellman[8] India has always accepted the physically handicapped; France gave the blind a place of privilege during the Middle Ages; the Eskimos left older persons to die. The ancient Greeks disposed of crippled children and believed the physically impaired were inferior. The pre-prophetic Hebrew believed that the sick were being punished by God while the early Christians believed that ministering to the handicapped lead to the acquisition of moral virtue. This latter attitude combined with the Calvinist assumption that the absence of material success resulting from disability is visible evidence of the lack of grace, the Darwinian theory of survival of the fittest, and the technical progress of the twentieth century have created incredible ambivalence in public attitudes.

---

[7]V. W. Von Hagen, *World of the Maya* (New York, New American Library, 1960), p. 102.

[8]W. Gellman.

Those attitudes have combined into an attitude which might be expressed by the statement "helping handicapped people is the Christian thing to do and I will do it because I am a good person, but 'they' after all are inferior and therefore objects of pity."

Professional fund raisers have abetted the process of offering "grace" to the general public by preying on their desire to help but maintain distance by giving money to "help someone" — somewhere else.

In general, most people feel helpless when confronted by a person with a disability. There is a feeling of pity and/or guilt because people recognize their own good fortune at being able and what rotten luck it is that someone else has been deprived of the usual share of abilities. There is the same awkwardness in dealing with another's loss of ability as there is in dealing with death — total loss. What can you say or do to help when someone has lost a loved one or has lost or lacks an ability to function? When the answer is not obvious, awkwardness ensues.

There is, however, usually a willingness on the part of "able people" to do something to correct the natural imbalance of justice which obviously shortchanged some people. In order to achieve the second half of the rehabilitation process — changing the environment to accept handicapped people — we all must develop more opportunities for all people to use their willingness to help in ways which will enable them to learn about the potential for handicapped individuals. We must then involve the "normal" members of society in creating an accepting environment for disabled people. Every human being has limitations and is handicapped in some way. However, some limitations are more acceptable than others.

Sixth Barrier — Communities Do Not Want People Who Have Problems

A community would never voluntarily choose to have large numbers of people who are poor, disabled, or old. It would choose able-bodied, industrious, creative men and women and well-behaved, charming children who are good students and have the potential to recreate their parents' idealized images of themselves. The community or established group will resist most strenuously integrating newcomers who are different and do not conform to accepted norms. It will, however, more willingly provide for those who are different but already part of their numbers.

To be old, to be poor, to be lacking in physical prowess or intellectual ability are not popular goals. It would be madness to make them popular to gain acceptance for handicapped people.

To be admired, to be respected, to be smart, to be successful, to be beautiful, to have enough material goods to satisfy one's needs are popular self-goals. It is necessary to recognize that some individuals have not had a choice in their level of intellectual or physical capacity due to environmental or genetic conditions. Each human being is unique and each has special needs. The normal members of the community can fulfill their own goals for self-fulfillment by creating equal opportunities for people with special needs. This simultaneously removes the obstacles which constitute handicapping conditions in the community. We then are involved in the second half of the rehabilitiation process — changing the community. Education alone does not change attitudes. Involvement with and continued exposure to people who are different does change attitudes.

Seventh Barrier — The Attitudes Held by Professional People Toward the Establishment

The dedicated people who are attracted to helping handicapped people frequently are nonsupportive or even hostile to the majority group — the establishment. There is often a special hostility reserved for the power structure — the influentials. Wealthy individuals or individuals who control the economic well-being of a community and the decision makers, elected and appointed officials, are the frequent targets for criticism and charges of "do nothing," "unconcerned," and "insensitive" by professionals whose goal is to improve the quality of life for disabled people. The first method considered for achieving social change in this field is more often "confrontation" rather than "education." If we want handicapped people to be understood, then we must treat with equal understanding those people in a position to effect change. A bridge needs to be built between individuals in the rehabilitation field and individuals in the community. Both groups are essential to the creation of developmental opportunities for people with problems.

Eighth Barrier — Negative Attitudes by Employers

Employers with negative attitudes which limit employment potential for disabled people have been identified as a special target for education. The President's Committee for Employment of the Handicapped reported in June 1975 that one out of ten handicapped people who had been trained in special workshops was unable to find employment

Ninth Barrier — Language

The language of the professional psychologist, social worker, and special education teacher is highly specialized jargon and, therefore, must be translated for public consumption, if professionals with languages of their own and the lay public are to understand both the problems and the possible solutions.

Tenth Barrier — Lack of Manpower and Resources Devoted to Changing the Community

There is failure among professionals in the rehabilitation field to recognize that changing the functioning ability of the disabled person is not enough to insure acceptance. Broad social and attitudinal changes must occur, and they will occur only when resources are devoted to facilitate the change and a discipline is created to effect that change.

This book is devoted to presenting an integrated though limited body of knowledge which is aimed at "treating the community" or teaching the community to be supportive and accepting of people with differences.

We can create legislation which protects the rights of all citizens. We can legislate the use of tax dollars which provide for the equalization of developmental opportunities. However, a free society cannot make a disabled person want to become able and cannot change people's attitudes through legislation.

Just as the disabled person has the right to choose to live in the mainstream of life, a nursing home, or an institution, non-disabled people have the right to like or dislike having handicapped people live and work next to them. The freedom to cling to one's prejudices is just as much a part of freedom of choice as the acceptance of the brotherhood of all mankind.

For true acceptance to occur, the choice of supporting equal opportunities for people must be a voluntary one.

The state or federal government can plunk a batch of disabled people down in a community, build a facility, hire a staff to conduct developmental programs and teach the disabled people how to look normal, and the community may still not accept them because it was not involved in the process of creating the change and the people "plunked down" were not part of their group.

The sense of commitment felt by professionals in the field can be passed on to influential people and the general public, but the public must be involved in developing and implementing the changes necessary for integration at the community level. Only then will each disabled person have the freedom to choose his way of life.

Chapter 3

HOW TO BEGIN CREATING CHANGE

Underlying Concepts and Techniques for Creating Change

THE function of creating change within the community has been given low priority by many professionals in the service delivery system for handicapped people. If we are to really make it possible for the handicapped person to live in the mainstream, it is not enough to change the handicapped person; we must change the community in which he lives.

According to Kurt Lewin,[1] change occurs by diminishing restraining forces and increasing "driving forces." Therefore, it is necessary to first identify both the restraining forces and the driving forces, and then develop strategies to diminish the restraining forces and create or increase the driving forces.

Lewin looked upon a level or phase of behavior as a balance of forces working in opposite directions.

The following are among the restraining forces to the integration of disabled people into the mainstream of life:

1. Negative attitudes by employers toward hiring handicapped people
2. Negative attitudes and feelings of residents in a specific neighborhood toward having a group home or small apartment building on the same block or nearby
3. Restrictive zoning ordinances
4. Lack of funds for community services

The driving forces for integration might be just the group of disabled people themselves, or an organization in the community committed to advocating the rights of disabled people, or an organization whose purpose is to provide residential alternatives, or the organization plus specially recruited support from a broad spectrum in the community.

---

[1]K. Lewin, *Principles of Topological Psychology* (New York, McGraw-Hill, 1966).

Benne and Birnbaum[2] suggest there are three major strategies for achieving change in any given pattern of behavior — increase the driving forces, decrease the restraining forces, or a combination of both.

When the first strategy is implemented, the tension level is most apt to increase; since restraining forces are not reduced and may very well increase under pressure to change.

Increased tension in the situation is likely to create more instability and unpredictability, and the likelihood of irrational responses to the change attempt increase. Confrontation, that is, the assumption that the group or community is morally wrong, as a first step usually increases resistance.

The alternative to confrontation directed toward creating open conflict (increasing driving forces without decreasing restraining forces) is education and involvement of the opposing forces, thus decreasing restraining forces by eliminating misconceptions. Attack against restraining forces can result in winning the battle (short term gain) but losing the war (creating understanding and support), but attack can also simply intensify restraining forces, thus losing both the battle and the war.

Man is a social being. He frequently resists change because it threatens his relative position in life. Education and the dissemination of information help to create change, but they are not enough to create significant change. Those people who knowingly or unknowingly create obstacles to the integration of disabled people into life in the community must become involved in the process of change. Their involvement and resulting increased understanding will decrease the restraining forces which inhibit change, but it would be naive to assume that it is only necessary to change the viewpoint of the opposition. First, most communities must build up driving forces to be more than just the disabled population, their families, and professionals. Only after all attempts at creating understanding through education fail, then attack in the form of legal confrontation is of course appropriate. It should not, however, be the first course of action in creating change.

---

[2]K. Benne and M. Birnbaum, *Organizational Behavior and Administration,* rev. ed. (Homewood, Illinois, Richard D. Irwin, Inc., 1965), pp. 952-959.

It is not difficult to build philosophical and financial support for expanding opportunities for disabled people to live in the mainstream of life; but unless that support is present, it becomes much more difficult to create change. The philosophical and financial support is a driving force. For example, when starting a group home for retarded adults, immediate neighbors who may have negative feelings will be a restraining force. It is therefore necessary to balance those negative voices with individuals who represent an even larger group in the community.

If an issue arises which permits the restraining forces to unite and organize resistance, even a minority might prohibit the establishment of residences for handicapped people.

In order to protect the rights of the even smaller minority of substantially disabled people, it is essential that "driving forces" be organized to help the disabled population integrate into the mainstream.

Saul Alinsky,[3] the famous community organizer, emphasizes the importance of people doing things themselves. He states, "It is the most common human reaction that successful attainment of objectives is much more meaningful to people who have achieved the objectives through their own efforts. The objective is never an end itself. The efforts that are exerted in the actual earning of the objective are part and parcel of the achievement itself. It is all one continuous process." Most people value those things most which required effort and sacrifice. This reaction occurs cross-culturally in all things. What we get by our own effort is really ours. It is a part of us, bound and knit through the experiences that we have had and shared in securing it.

Alinsky goes on to say that, "There is a more profound basis for the passionate desire of all human beings to feel that they have personally contributed to the creation and the securing of any objective they desire. It is a part of what great religious schools of thought call the dignity of man."

In our experience, assistance granted grudgingly is better than no assistance at all, but assistance given voluntarily leaves

---

[3]S. Alinsky, *Revielle for Radicals* (New York, Random House, 1969).

the giver happier and accomplishes the desired goal for the beneficiary.

By advocating and subsequently demonstrating that handicapped people can indeed live in the mainstream of life and that the majority can become productive members of society, we can relieve a massive amount of public guilt.

By giving the public the opportunity to help handicapped people by creating opportunities for development, a formerly negative feeling can be changed to a positive one.

Give the public a way to help as individuals and in groups, and their acceptance and understanding will magnify enormously. Then communicate how Mr. Jones, the businessman; Mrs. Smith, the housewife; Mrs. Philip, the senior citizen; Mr. Samson, the construction worker; Mrs. Jones, the realtor; Miss Green, the secretary; Mr. Butler, the corporation president; Dr. Brown, the pediatrician; Mrs. Wegner, the socialite; and Bobby Porter, the athlete, have each helped.

Constant publicity on what direct services are available, what needs are still unmet, and what handicapped people are doing in a positive way, are all valuable. But each person identifies with his own peers and when he reads about and talks to those who are involved, then his own interest and support heightens.

By involving the real "leaders" and establishment in the community we can accelerate the change process. Who are the leaders (mayor, bank president, wealthy citizens, politically influential people) and "movers and shakers" (those people who can act as catalysts to move things along)? When leaders work along with the existing constituency on one project their increased level of awareness regarding the special problems and potential of disabled people generates far-reaching interest, concern, involvement, and support. It is necessary to involve local elected officials to eliminate restrictive zoning codes. Negative attitudes of employers change through "peer" education. These individuals, as well as the disabled people, their families, and professionals in the field, provide voices which put into perspective the voices of a dissident few. Advocates and supporters can also help deal with a primary concern of community agencies — the need for more financial support.

Interestingly, fund-raising events can often be the kickoff point for more extensive involvement and the funds raised can be used to expand the community education program, as well as provide voluntary dollars for other services. The expanded public education generates more interest and involvement and thereby more dollars. The answer to the question of who will pay for the community education program is "the public education program pays for itself many times over."

All that needs to be done is to set the mechanism for generating and receiving contributions in motion, but, and this is a critical but, the money raised must be asked for not to increase pity but rather as an investment in the development of human potential right here! *Fund raising can and should be used as a tool in the social process of integration.*

A single special event can bring people together to achieve a common purpose. It acts as the basis for the agency, its staff and constituency, to learn more about the influentials and decision makers in the community as people. At the same time the influential people learn about the agency programs and its constituency, including handicapped clients themselves. The dynamics of people learning about people is reciprocal.

The awe or cynicism many people feel about those in a position to exert authority is diminished when they meet eyeball to eyeball in a living room. At a public hearing, public officials are frequently seated on a dais with high desks separating them from the petitioner seeking assistance or support. The social situation removes the visible inhibiting barriers of petitioner versus public official.

Influentials are people who are in a position to control all or part of the economic well-being of a community. They are powerful because they have real influence in the outcome of decisions. Some influentials have limited personal wealth but exert influence because they distribute money or control jobs. Political influentials may be elected or appointed. Therefore the influence may be interrupted by the election process. Individuals who possess significant personal wealth are most apt to remain influential because they can control more of the circumstances which make them influential.

Effective communication takes place when distortions are minimized and the opportunity for feedback to each communicator is maximized.

An important point to make in creating acceptance is that members of the dominant social group, members of the minority group, and arbitrators are all people. As we each learn more about each other, prejudices and preconceived ideas melt. The lay public, officials, and influential people may have prejudices and misconceptions about handicapped people, but professionals in the rehabilitation field, handicapped clients, and their parents also have prejudices about the public, officials, and influential people. The more interaction each group has with the other, the more acceptance will take place. Prejudice is multidimensional. Barriers are multidimensional. Receptivity must be multidimensional.

The Prince by Machiavelli, 1513

> There is nothing more difficult to carry out, nor more doubtful of success, nor more dangerous to handle, than to initiate a new order of things. For the reformer has enemies in all who profit by the old order, and only lukewarm defenders in all those who profit by the new order. This lukewarmness arises partly from fear of their adversaries who have law in their favor, and partly from the incredulity of mankind, who do not truly believe in anything new until they have actual experience of it.

SECTION II
The Plan

Chapter 4

COMMUNITY EDUCATION, ORGANIZATION, AND INVOLVEMENT LEAD TO SOCIAL ACTION AND ACCEPTANCE

As we move away from caring for disabled people in institutions and toward the development of ways to help disabled people in their own communities, it is essential that an extensive social action plan be implemented at the community level to facilitate the integration of the disabled population into the mainstream of community life.

According to the National Association of Superintendents of Public Residential Facilities for the Mentally Retarded, deinstitutionalization consists of three interrelated components: (1) prevention of admission by finding and developing alternative community methods of care and training, (2) return to the community *all* residents who have been prepared through programs of habilitation, rehabilitation, and training to live in appropriate local settings, and (3) establishment and maintenance of a responsive residential environment which protects human and civil rights and which contributes to the expeditious return of the individual to normal community living, whenever possible.[1]

In "A Model for Deinstitutionalization,"[2] Scheerenberger states that a successful program of deinstitutionalization will require institutional reform, community reform, juridical reform, and legislative reform. He says that institutions must work with community service delivery systems to facilitate the

---

[1]National Association of Superintendents of Public Residential Facilities for the Mentally Retarded, 1974, pp. 4-5.

[2]R. C. Scheerenberger. "A Model for Deinstitutionalization," *Mental Retardation, 12* (6), December 1974, p. 6.

movement of disabled people into the mainstream.

Scheerenberger also says that the broad community, outside the service delivery system, must express a greater willingness to include disabled people in the mainstream of everyday life. The juridical system must recognize and protect the rights of the disabled and respond to existing inequities with alacrity. Legislators, at both state and national levels, also must recognize and protect the rights of handicapped people and provide those laws and resources necessary to enable them to live as full and rich a life as possible within the total society.[3] A good deal of attention has been devoted to creating change through legislation and this effort is well-directed. However, only minimal efforts have been made to effect change at the community level. National and statewide public education programs have evolved with varying degrees of sophistication and have created attitudinal change at the philosophical level. However, the action is at the community level and very few organizations have created a program to achieve the second half of the rehabilitation process — removing the conditions which are handicapping to disabled individuals in the community.

If we are intent on effecting normalization, the steps necessary for social action must begin by (1) broadening the targets for community education and involvement to all members of the community, (2) developing a plan for organizing and educating the community, (3) developing mechanisms to involve the community in achieving the social changes necessary to integrate disabled people into the community, and of extreme importance, (4) specifically enlisting the support of influential people and decision makers in the community to achieve the established goals.

The organization which most aggressively and willingly initiates the social action program reaps the benefit of the community's voluntary dollars.

Broadening the Target for Community Education

Traditionally, agencies serving mentally retarded and physi-

---

[3]R. C. Scheerenberger.

cally handicapped people were started and run by parents and have evolved into professionally run agencies geared to providing day-care programs for varying levels and ages of people. The expansion of services from day care into comprehensive developmental programs which provide residential alternatives other than institutionalization has created an urgent need to create an atmosphere of understanding, awareness, and acceptance in the community. Social change begins by communicating the need for change and then evolves through action and reaction.

The traditional channels of communication regarding disabilities have been agencies organized to help disabled people, such as associations for retarded citizens, united cerebral palsy groups, epilepsy organizations — in general, membership groups of parents, educators, and social service professionals (physicians, legislators, and attorneys).

These traditional target populations comprise probably 12 to 15 percent of our total population.

Outside the circle of parents, professionals, and legislators, public attitude toward retarded or developmentally disabled people can best be described as one of avoidance. One verbalization of the public feeling is "It upsets me to see someone visibly handicapped, so I don't want to look." In the case of a hidden disability such as epilepsy it might be said, "I don't know what a seizure is, and I don't know what to do if someone has one, so I don't want to be near one who has it." In the case of mental illness and reaction frequently is "I don't understand what it is, but he acts funny and I don't know how to react to that, and furthermore, I'm afraid he might hurt me or my children." Many fund raising efforts have perpetuated this public stance to the detriment of creating positive feelings toward handicapped people. The fund raising appeals using pity — "Won't you give some money to help these poor people find a little love and a place to stay?" — or guilt — "We *must* help these children." — are dehumanizing and in fact defeat the goal of integration. United Fund appeals tend to reduce information in regard to handicapped people, substituting bland generalizations.

Public apathy and avoidance can be changed, but it requires

an understanding of the art of communication and the skills used in that art. The United States certainly harbors a vast majority of the "public communications talent" in the world. If an advertising campaign can persuade thousands of people to buy cereal or soap, then those same techniques can be used to communicate (1) the need for acceptance of developmentally disabled people, (2) the contributing role handicapped people can play in society, (3) the rights of all citizens, including the handicapped, to live, work, and play in the mainstream of life. Attitudinal changes occur when people not only learn but experience through constant exposure and involvement. The key to involvement is identifying the role each individual can play in helping, e.g. the individual can be encouraged to do the following:

a. Be a volunteer. Devote time outside usual activities to actively help.
b. Employ handicapped people.
c. Provide subcontract work for workshop training programs.
d. Support equal opportunities — fight discrimination.
e. Provide financial support.
f. Be an advocate, either within the framework of everyday activities or in addition to normal activities; do what you can when the occasion arises to help eliminate handicapping conditions.

Just as we strive to teach the disabled person to be socially acceptable to the general public, so we can make helping handicapped people become the socially acceptable cause.

A Plan for Organizing and Educating the Community

The first step in creating opportunities for handicapped people to live, work, learn, and play in the mainstream of life, is to provide a system for disseminating information and for

[4]Accreditation Council for Facilities for the Mentally Retarded, Joint Commission on Accreditation of Hospitals, *Standards for Community Agencies Serving Persons with Mental Retardation and Other Developmental Disabilities*, Chicago, Joint Committee on Accreditation of Hospitals, 1973

providing opportunities for the involvement of people at every level in every community — national, state, county, municipality, and neighborhood — to help in creating the changes necessary. As stated in the standards for community education and involvement in the *Standards of Community Agencies Serving Persons with Mental Retardation and Other Developmental Disabilities*[4] written by the Accreditation Council for Facilities for the Mentally Retarded, Joint Commission on Accreditation of Hospitals, each agency in cooperation with other agencies involved in providing services to handicapped people should conduct an ongoing community education program that is designed to create community awareness and acceptance of mentally retarded and other developmentally disabled persons. Their community education program should focus on communicating what services they provide and how they help handicapped people. Specific attention needs to be focused on understanding the general and special needs of the disabled, and on the right of disabled citizens to participate in the mainstream of community life. Each agency should, therefore, establish a fixed point for collecting and disseminating information within the agency or cooperatively with other agencies.

Each agency needs a procedure for disseminating information during a crisis. The chief executive officer and one appointed spokesman can usually solve the problem of "who knows the whole story."

Each agency can participate in making the community aware of the causes of mental retardation and other developmental disabilities and whatever other handicapping conditions they serve. It should also educate the general public concerning community programs that are available and needs that remain unmet. You are, however, competing for attention. Be honest but dramatize. Stir emotions to gain attention initially, then get to the second level of informing by developing the tools necessary to communicate:

Detailed brochures on services currently provided, freely distributed;

Detailed fact sheets describing program components;

Regularly mailed newsletters to members of a constituency;

Audio-visual materials such as film and slide presentations;
A speakers' bureau;
Program presentations, meetings, and seminars;
School and college class presentations;
A total media publicity program, including press releases, staff interviews, and consumer interviews;
A library and bibliography of books and publications for staff, parents, and the general public.

It is essential that special informational sessions for special audiences, such as public and private officials, be conducted on the advantages to the community and to disabled people when normalized living arrangements are made available for disabled people in the community. These are designed to support the adoption of zoning ordinances that promote normalization and support the adoption of licensing standards that promote normalization; focus on communicating what services they provide and how they help handicapped people. Specific attention needs to be focused on understanding the general and special needs of the disabled, and on the right of disabled citizens to participate in the mainstream of community life. Each agency should, therefore, establish a fixed point for collecting and disseminating information within the agency or cooperatively with other agencies.

The National Association for Retarded Citizens, United Cerebral Palsy, and The Epilepsy Foundation of America develop TV spots with celebrities for public service announcements. The state associations in many instances develop public information materials applicable to the situation in that state, but the local agency is dealing with the front lines. There is, indeed, a difference between the philosophy of equality and having someone who is different move in next door. The need for change is directly dependent on the degree of acceptance and support for handicapped people in that locale. That acceptance can be measured by the ease with which handicapped people fit into the normal classroom and find employment and the availability of appropriate residential alternatives. The latter would include the freedom to choose a residence based on each individual's need or wants, anything from total independence in one's own home or apartment, to a supervised group home or apartment setting, to life in a residential environment which has nursing services available, to total nursing care. When employment opportunities are freely available and a variety of residential services are in operation which permit the disabled person to choose the residential life-style which best meets his needs, the need for community education de-escalates. Community education is an advocacy function. Its purpose is to provide an environment in which people with special needs can function as fully as possible.

These efforts must be coordinated, but they must also provide each service agency with the freedom to express its own philosophy and use its own approach in educating and in changing the obstacles in each community, primarily because each local community is unique and responds differently to different approaches.

The goals, however, of all agencies at all levels are uniform — creating an atmosphere of understanding and awareness to maximize opportunities for handicapped people to develop to the highest level of competency possible.

1. Discover the causes of various disabilities and means of preventing them.
2. Develop awareness of the needs and potentials of disabled people.
3. Publicize the existence of developmental services and how they create change in the functioning level of disabled people.
4. Describe the ways in which the so-called "normal" population can help handicapped people become more independent and integrate into the mainstream of life.

Education can help decrease restraining forces by replacing myths, but talking is not enough. Education is not enough. While restraining forces may never be completely eliminated, they can be further diminished by involving individuals who resist change in actually planning the process for implementing change. Involve the opposition.

Developing Mechanisms to Involve the Community

Driving forces can be created or increased by the presentation of opportunities for the involvement of people and organizations in all stratas of society to effect change in both disabled persons and the environment by (1) involving professionals, individuals, and organizations in the rehabilitation and educational fields, as well as all related social and medical specialties through a planned program under the direction of a qualified staff; and (2) involving the general public by providing opportunities for participation in effecting change. (In order to communicate and involve the lay community, the "lingo" of the physician, psychiatrist, psychologist, special educator, and social worker must be replaced with the language which most clearly and simply expresses the rationale for permitting handicapped people to live in the mainstream of life.)

The mechanism available to motivate people to accept handicapped peers as equals is circular, i.e. the needs of handicapped people are met by meeting the self-fulfillment and ego needs of normal people through providing them with the opportunity to help handicapped people. In this way, we acquaint normal people with individuals and groups with whom they have formerly been uncomfortable.

Abraham Maslow evolved the concept of a hierarchy of human needs, stating that a person must first satisfy his own physiological needs, then safety needs, then social needs, and eventually ego and self-fulfillment needs. Professor Douglas McGregor pointed out that modern industry (and indeed modern life) offers only limited opportunities for the satisfaction of ego needs for people. As our society has become more mobile, with large numbers of people needing to satisfy social needs — the need for belonging, for association, for acceptance by one's fellow man, for giving and receiving love — self-fulfillment needs remain largely unmet. Unlike the lower needs, the need for self-fulfillment is rarely fully satisfied.

If the philosophical concept of "helping handicapped people develop to their maximum level of competence while living in the mainstream of life" is socially acceptable, then those people who give help, in their own way, to achieve that goal, have the opportunity to improve their own feelings of self-esteem. This applies to the physician who works with the director of a program for developmentally disabled infants and their mothers; he must communicate with his peers the value of using both a medical and a developmental prescription to help a disabled child grow and learn as part of his family. It also applies to the homemaker who does volunteer work in an office, or the business person who chairs a fund raising drive or special event, or the employer who hires handicapped people and is ultimately persuaded to make his place of business an on-the-job training site for disabled workers.

As stated in the Joint Commission Standards,[5] community involvement is obtained by methods that include but are not necessarily limited to the following:

Using volunteers in the community education program;
Involving citizens in writing and contacting their legislators in support of needed legislation;
Sponsoring special events that appeal to broad community interests in support of program needs;
Conducting activities that express and recognize citizen support of program needs;
Recognizing community leaders for their participation in and support of new program developments;
Encouraging fraternal, civic, and social organizations to support programs for the mentally retarded and other developmentally disabled;
Encouraging organizations to invite the mentally retarded and other disabled people to become members and to participate in activities with their peers.

All plans for involvement of people in the community should be designed to reward both the volunteer and the program for handicapped people.

If the involvement results in positive feelings, interest will be maintained and a larger and larger base of support can be built. It is interesting that most rehabilitation agencies serving handicapped people have a staff-to-client ratio of anywhere from 1-1 to 1-10. The staff-to-public ratio is more often one staff person to the total community, if that. In a large agency such as the

[5]Accreditation Council for Facilities for the Mentally Retarded, Joint Commission on Accreditation of Hospitals.

Ray Graham Association for the Handicapped, which serves over 800 clients a year and has 125 staff members, 3 staff members devote full-time to public education, volunteer involvement, and the development of local funding support. Three more full-time staff members work on contract procurement and job placement. Based on Ray Graham's performance record, with a ratio of 6 staff members to 300,000 people in the community, substantial interaction with and support from the community can be achieved. How many agencies devote even 1 full-time staff member for every 50,000 members of the general public? With the growing emphasis on "normalization" it is time to recognize that community education and community involvement deserve a separate professional discipline directed toward the second half of the rehabilitation process — eliminating handicapping conditions in the community. Every agency should develop a program and staff if it is to be successful in moving handicapped people into the mainstream of life. The need for community development must be moved to higher priority if we are to effect change.

Just as the functioning ability of the disabled person is improved under the direction of a specially trained staff, so can the community's ability to assimilate and support the needs of disabled people be improved. Change will not occur unless a specially trained staff develops the resources of the community. A community education and development staff treats the community as the client — the entity in need of change. The Appendix describes the staff and activities required to treat the community.

Donald J. Stedman, Director of the National Developmental Disabilities Technical Assistance System, in *Advocacy: A Role for Developmental Disabilities Councils*[6] says, "Without passion, the energy and persistence required to work daily against the resistance to change and progress for the disabled is not possible. The enthusiasm necessary to generate new strength and determination in others cannot be communicated without the caring and sensible devotion to the task. Passion makes the

---

[6]D. J. Stedman, *Advocacy: A Role for Developmental Disabilities Councils*, monograph edited by J. L. Paul, R. Wiegerink, and G. R. Newfeld, 1974, p. 212.

small gains satisfying."

However, Stedman goes on, "Without the knowledge, skill, data, facts, and understanding of problems and their solutions, all the passion in the world will never help the developmentally disabled."

Chapter 5

DESIGNING AND STAFFING A COMMUNITY EDUCATION AND DEVELOPMENT PROGRAM

THE goal of a community education and development program is to create an atmosphere of understanding and awareness for disabled people so that they may function as fully as possible in the mainstream of the community.

The purposes of a community education and development program are threefold. The first responsibility is to communicate the special needs and potential of disabled people, the existence of services for disabled people so that those who need the services may avail themselves of them, the need for services not yet available, the need for changing conditions which are handicapping to disabled people, the need for support — philosophical, volunteer, and financial. The second responsibility is to design the most effective way to create an atmosphere favorable to maximize the normalized living of disabled people in the community. The third responsibility of the program is to generate the needed philosophical, volunteer, and financial support in order to bring about the necessary changes.

The program staff reporting directly to the executive director of a direct service or advocacy agency should be headed by a director of community education and development or director of development. In a small agency, the executive director might prefer to assume the development role. In order to allocate time to that role it would probably be necessary to appoint a director of programming or director of operations for other agency activities consuming time and subject to many demands.

Since the purpose of the community education and development program for agencies serving handicapped people is to create change, fund raising is not an end in itself, *it is only a tool* — albeit a powerful and flexible one.

The director of development, as an official spokesman for the agency, is charged with the responsibility of communicating with the general public and with specific groups outside the service delivery system. He reports directly to the executive director and works with the executive director and the direct program staff in discussing priorities which should be established regarding needed changes. After decisions by the governing body of the organization regarding goals and priorities, the director of development designs the means for communicating, creating change, and generating support.

The director of development or executive director ideally should be able to attain recognition and acceptance by the power structure of the local community.

The staff person(s) assigned under the director to communicate with the community and stimulate people to get involved in helping handicapped people should be selected by personality and organizational skills rather than by educational background. An outgoing, catalytic personality, an appreciation for people as individuals, a capacity to organize and manage, and an ability to communicate effectively would be basic requirements. Experience and the ability to motivate people to achieve a common goal is essential. Age, sex, and professional training are of secondary importance. In some ways, graduate training in the field of special education, psychology, or rehabilitation may be a limiting condition since the pattern of professionalized language must be changed back to the language of common use in the community.

The ability to cut through to the essence of a program and communicate it succinctly and simply is a skill which can be learned, but it is more economic if it is already evident when an applicant is interviewed.

The preparation and dissemination of all public educational materials, setting up lines of communication, and establishing the means whereby community acceptance and involvement can be created and implemented are the primary responsibilities of a community education program.

Similarly, as the community education coordination staff

interacts with the community and interest is established, follow-up should be assigned to the appropriate staff person.

If the grandmother of a handicapped child approaches the community education coordinator regarding the availability of services, the community education coordinator can get grandmother's name and number and have the intake social worker call the family. If a businessman indicates interest in having the agency bid on subcontract work, the community education coordinator should take his name and have the person in charge of contract procurement call. If a school psychologist asks for more information about the program, his name should be given to the appropriate professional staff to follow up. The community education coordinator acts as a catalyst and liaison, and whenever possible passes contact on to the staff person specifically responsible for that kind of involvement in direct service.

Since acceptance of handicapped people is the goal, the background of this staff person should really be compatible with the culture, educational level, and social community in which he will be working.

A long standing, well-accepted member of the community is ideal. An individual who is familiar with the community or comes from a similar one would be good. Someone from the inner city trying to relate to a rural community would have a difficult time. The wife of a farmer would be a good choice in a farming community, while a suburban matron working in an inner city Latino community would have difficulty. A black Ph.D. would have a hard time relating to Alleghany poor. It is not impossible for someone with a totally different background; it is just more difficult and may take longer to achieve goals, because there is even more learning which must take place for both the staff person and the community. Establishing credibility is dependent upon having a trust relationship between spokesman and community.

The accepted, respected member of the community who says this is what is happening and this is what needs to be done, already has the confidence of his peers, which lends legitimacy to his proposals. The accepted member is himself a legitimator.

His friends help because they know "Charlie" and they trust his judgment. They do not have to spend a great deal of time developing a trust relationship.

Small, well-defined communities present a totally different challenge from the large city where individual identities are unknown next door, let alone a mile away. However, even the densely populated cities have identifiable communities within them. One four-square-mile area might have five or ten distinct communities with differing ethnic backgrounds, educational, social, and economic levels. The farmer's wife would not know where to start but an outgoing city-bred person would.

A large part of the success of an agent of change is due to knowing who to work with and how the change can be effected. The long-time resident, active member of the community knows or can easily find out who the decision makers are and who the influential people are behind the decision makers for each situation. The individuals who have formal authority for a specific area are not necessarily always the people who decide what will or will not happen. The larger the community, the more complex and multilayered are the mechanisms with which one must deal.

Just as financial support is a resource, so volunteers are a resource which should be developed. The volunteer coordinator on the community education staff needs to be able to match the talents of people in the community with the needs of handicapped people and programmatic goals. Volunteers cannot always articulate what they can do best.

The community education staff will be dealing with a tremendous number of people with greatly differing needs: the bank vice-president who wants constant newspaper exposure for his activities; the beautiful woman who has been stigmatized by her beauty and wants others to know she cares about others more than about the way she looks; the homemaker whose children are leaving the nest and who needs to be needed by someone or something else; the wife and mother who does not have enough confidence in her abilities to look for paid employment; the highly successful executive who may have been extremely aggressive and lucky in climbing the ladder to success and has come to feel the need to share his newly acquired resources with others; the disabled person who has worked very hard to relate to nondisabled people by literally ignoring his disability, has achieved success, and has realized that he wants to help other disabled people. All of these are potential volunteers.

These are just a few examples of people with very real unsatisfied needs who can help to educate the community and create the changes which will make the environment more livable for disabled people. While volunteers are helping handicapped people, they are also helping themselves grow and are satisfying their own needs. The community education staff must perceive the needs or wants of members of the community and then channel those needs into the service structure to assist disabled people.

The community educator plays the role of initial contactor and catalyst; a volunteer coordinator is the person who sees that the individual's or group's talents are utilized effectively in satisfying programmatic needs as well as individual volunteer needs.

As the community education program develops, the staff roles can then be split into four separate specialities:

1. Director of development and community education;
2. The public speaker and involver — community development coordinator;
3. The writer preparing all written public information material, audio-visual presentations, communication through mass media — community educator coordinator;
4. Coordinator of volunteer resources for both direct services and indirect services — volunteer coordinator.

Following are job descriptions for the roles of director of development, community education coordinator, and volunteer coordinator. Also following is a brief chart indicating the five-year evolution of the Ray Graham Association's community education program as a reference for planning.

Sample Job Description

Position: Director of Development
Responsible to: Executive Director
Function: The Director of Development is charged with creating an atmosphere of understanding and awareness in the community to enhance the opportunity for disabled people to function as fully as possible in the mainstream of the community, and with developing the resources needed.

The responsibilities of the Director of Development include directing and designing a program to educate the community regarding the needs of disabled people, the services offered by this organization, the need for the establishment of services, and the goals of the organization as determined by the board of directors.

In order to carry out the goals of the organization, the Director of Development will design, recommend, and, on approval from the Board of Directors and Executive Director, implement a program for community development and support.

The following activities should be included in the duties of the Director of Development:

1. Supervision of the Community Education Coordinator on the preparation of all public information materials to be released to the public, designing channels of communication as well as the most effective means of communication.
2. Supervising the Community Development Coordinator in designing the means to achieve needed changes in the community, including organizing and involving the general public in implementing the changes and working with both local units of government and local individuals and organizations to eliminate discriminating laws and codes as they apply to handicapped people.
3. Supervising the Volunteer Coordinator in designing the best means of utilizing volunteers in both direct service and indirect service programs.
4. Designing and implementing the means for generating

financial support from the community for both operational income in services and for capital purposes; all fund raising to be conducted within the guidelines of fund-raising policies and goals established by the board of directors.

5. Have direct responsibility in fund-raising activities of the legal governing bodies with regard to operations and for capital purposes. Provide technical assistance to the Volunteer League Board (Women's Auxiliary) and supervision for the Volunteer Coordinator who will have the direct staff relationship in fund-raising activities of the Volunteer League. Provide technical assistance to the community education and development staff in generating contributions through individuals and clubs and organizations in the community.
6. Supervise the collection and preparation of all data for accountability to the community.
7. Supervise the preparation of all grant requests to Community Chests, local units of government, i.e. township review sharing and County Planning Commission, and private foundations and major individual donors.
8. Select the appropriate staff and volunteers for each presentation.
9. Act as official spokesman for the agency at the direction of the Executive Director. Provide consultation on issues relating to all agency "positions" on policy for release to the public.
10. Act as consultant in establishing procedures for the dissemination of information during a crisis.
11. Under the direction of the Executive Director, work with state and federal legislators regarding the needs of their handicapped constituents in the agency's service area and the implications of pending state and federal legislation as it affects handicapped citizens and the organization.
12. Work with elected officials and local units of government to collect data on the needs of handicapped citizens to effect a county-wide planning effort to meet the needs of those individuals.

13. Coordinate the acquisition of all real property to be used for the operation of direct service programs by working with the Director of the Direct Service Program utilizing the property, realtors to identify potential sites, real estate investment consultants, appraisers, local governmental units, and attorneys for legal advice in executing acquisition and financing.
14. Provide staff assistance as a Director of the Foundation for the Handicapped in all its activities.

Sample Job Description

Position: Volunteer Coordinator
Responsible to: Director of Development
Function: The Volunteer Coordinator is responsible for the following:

1. The recruitment and assignment of volunteers matching the program needs with the abilities and needs of the volunteers in groups and as individuals.
2. The orientation and general training of volunteers regarding the agency and its policies.
3. Maintaining accurate records with regard to volunteer name, address, phone number, family status, special talents, and availability in terms of hours.
4. Working with the direct service program staff to assure the volunteer is receiving instruction in his expected role and in recording hours worked by each volunteer.
5. Working cooperatively with the Community Education Coordinator on indirect service volunteers.
6. Granting special recognition of outstanding contributions by volunteer help.

Sample Job Description

Position: Community Education Coordinator
Responsible to: Director of Development
Function: The Community Education staff is responsible for the following duties in regards to the goal of community education:

1. Communication with the general public and constituency of the Association in the geographical area served by the Association.
2. The preparation and dissemination of all public education materials.
3. Relations with mass media and the preparation and dissemination of all materials to be released through the media upon approval of the Executive Director and Director of Development.
4. The operation of a speakers' bureau utilizing articulate staff members, including the Community Education Coordinator, to stimulate understanding and awareness of the Agency's programs and the needs of handicapped people.
5. Assembling all data regarding the Association for release to the public.

The Community Education Coordinator has certain responsibilities in the area of community development:

1. The maintenance of communication and relations with clubs, organizations, and individuals interested in the welfare of handicapped people and in the activities of the Association.
2. Conducting or coordinating agency-wide tours of facilities for interested individuals and organizations.
3. Structuring the means by which interested members of the community can help create an atmosphere in the community which will enhance the quality of life for handicapped people.
4. Maintaining all records of support in the form of contributions of money, goods, and participation in projects.

Chapter 6

EVALUATION AND EVOLUTION OF A COMMUNITY EDUCATION PROGRAM

Chapter 6

EVALUATION AND EVOLUTION OF A COMMUNITY EDUCATION PROGRAM

The Ray Graham Association community education/involvement staff evolved as follows and can be measured for its impact based on the following criteria:

	1969	1970-71	1971-72	1972-73	1973-74	1974-75	1975-76
Staff	No staff position	Community Education Coordinator	Community Education Coordinator, part-time secretary	Community Education Coordinator, full-time secretary	Community Education Coordinator, assistant secretary	Community Education Coordinator	Director of Development, secretary, Community Education Coordinator, secretary, Volunteer Coordinator, part-time secretary
People served by agency (approximately):	120	150	200	300	500	700	800
People placed on jobs:	8	17	20	30	50	80	105
Community tax support for operations:					25,000	146,156	178,663
Community voluntary contributions for operations:	36,724	88,978	129,561	137,896	146,091	154,764	297,073
Community voluntary contributions for capital:				11,753	28,559	77,831	55,234
Total budget of agency	188,836	581,576	788,257	1,126,502	1,414,431	1,834,037	2,510,594
Residential alternatives developed:				First community living facility started	Community living facility and independent apartments	Community living facility and independent group home and independent apartments and funding established to build specialized living center for severely disabled needing medical supervision	Two community living facilities – independent apartments – children's developmental home, specialized living center architect's plan developed, land acquired, money allocated $3,000,000. Funding established through state housing authority for special training residence for intellectually alert, physically handicapped people, $600,000.
Other programs started				One early infant program	Two early infant programs	Four early infant programs	

In retrospect, it would be better to plan that:	1 YR.	2 YR.	3 YR.	4 YR.	5 YR.
Staff:	Have Community Education Coordinator and full-time secretary	Hire Director of Development, secretary, Community Education Coordinator, part-time secretary	Director of Development, secretary, Community Education Coordinator, Volunteer Coordinator, secretary	Director of Development, secretary, Community Education Coordinator, secretary, Volunteer Coordinator, secretary, Public Information Coordinator	Director of Development, secretary, Community Education Coordinator, secretary, Volunteer Coordinatory, Public Information Coordinator, secretary
Objectives:	Meet immediate needs – start lines of communication, begin public education, establish need, establish ways for involvement.	Meet immediate needs and plan for next year begin working with power structure to legitimate need, continue communication, continue public education, implement means of involvement.	Begin long-range planning, formalize involvement of power structure to create commitment, continue education and means of involvement.	Activate involvement of power structure, expand use of mass media in education efforts, professional public information staff needed because of increased visibility.	

The way in which our own community education program has unfolded and its effect on the growth of services available for disabled people might serve as a guide to organizations weighing the relative merits of investing in a specific community education staff person versus direct service program staff. Adequate staff must be available to deal with the community once the program starts having impact. During growth periods, additional staff is required. When growth levels off, staff can be cut back somewhat.

Chapter 7

RECORD KEEPING

Records Needed for Community Accountability

I. Information Needed on Clients For Community Education Record Keeping As A Base For Presentations to Local Nonprofessional Funding Sources

1. Name (Total confidentiality: If accountability is required by community funding sources on a contract for services base, use initials and address only, if possible; for other purposes, to present an unduplicated account of individuals served in each community use birthdate, initials, and community, i.e. 9/1/36 RN Elmhurst.
2. Client's address
3. Township
4. Town, state
5. Telephone number
6. Disability
7. Date entered program
8. Name of program
9. Date left program — Where to?
10. Re-entry dates
11. Parents' names
12. Parents' addresses

    The problem of accountability and client confidentiality often seems in conflict on community accountability, especially to nonprofessional funding sources. Revenue sharing contracts for service agreements frequently require identification of individuals to insure they are residents of the city, county, or township doing the contracting. Community Chests will usually treat their support as a gift rather than a contract for service and require only data on the number of people served in each program from each community and the total number of hours served along with budgetary information.

II. Above Information for Community Education Record Keeping Will Be Used For

1. Revenue sharing fund requests and agreements (initials, address, town, township, program)
2. Community Chest applications (number of clients in each program in each community)

Records Needed for Members, Volunteers, Contributors — in Establishing a Constituency List for Communication

I. Information Needed for Contributors, All Categories, Posted On Individual Contribution Cards

1. Individual's name
2. Organization or corporate name
3. Address
4. Town, state, zip code
5. Telephone number
6. Amount given — date of each gift (month, day, year)
7. Code identifying type of contribution (M — membership; G — gift; CC — Christmas Cards; SS — special events, Patrons, Angels, ticket buyers; A — advertiser; P — parent; C — client)

II. Address Label System Needed For

1. Thank you letters
2. Newsletters
3. Annual reports
4. Fund raising or follow-up solicitations where appropriate

III. Above Information Will Be Used For

1. Annual report listings (contributors and members names unless anonymity is requested)
2. Mailing newsletters
3. Fund-raising solicitation
4. Notification of special events, meetings, happenings, need for letter writing, etc.

Chapter 8

UNDERSTANDING ATTITUDES

NEGATIVE attitudes toward people who are different from the dominant culture cause individuals who are members of the minority group to experience feelings ranging from being exotic and therefore interesting, to being an outsider, to being blatantly rejected.

Xenophobia

Xenophobia — Greek for "fear of the stranger" and "welcome to my house" — accurately reflects the ambivalence one feels toward someone who is different. In a Judeo-Christian ethic people know they *should* accept people who have made mistakes (ex-convicts) or people who had more problems than they can cope with (alcoholics, drug addicts, and the mentally ill). They also know it is not the retarded person's fault that he is retarded. They know they *should not* turn away from someone who is visibly severely handicapped, but the reality is, many people *feel* threatened by the presence of these persons, especially when they are in groups in their midst. When the numbers of such people are small the threat is smaller. When the group is large the threat is greater.

Continued personal rejection of the handicapped person reinforces the individual's fear that he is inferior or "not able." This is clearly a significant problem because it intensifies a damaged self-image which intensifies the disability. Neither this continued rejection nor the abuse of civil rights as in refusing employment, housing opportunities, or education can be tolerated.

Those attitudes must be changed. In many instances negative attitudes are the basis for rejection. Changing anything requires understanding. Therefore, in dealing with attitudes let us consider the following:

1. Attitudes which reflect expectations of inferior performance or deviate behavior.
2. Attitudes relating to the characteristic each individual most fears acquiring for self.
3. The amount of social distance each individual wants from people or groups possessing a degree of differentness that is discomforting or threatening.
4. What people say their attitudes are.
5. That these expressed attitudes may be in conflict with their real feelings.
6. The effect involvement has on changing attitudes.

Attitudes Which Reflect Expectations of Inferior Performance

Harasymiw, Horne, Lewis, and Baron[1] presented a paper at the Annual International Exceptional Children Convention in Chicago, April 1976. They pointed out the effect which negative attitudes held by special education teachers and the children's peers can have on handicapped children. The handicapped child in the classroom subjected to the possibly prejudiced attitudes of teachers and peers might be more prone to arrive at a lower self-evaluation, which in turn could lead to lowered work output and further decreased self-evaluation. This cyclical and mutually reinforcing system of devaluation could consequently impair future growth since individuals often behave in a manner consistent with their self-appraisal. A student who has the self-perception of "failure" is less likely to continue striving, thus precluding continued self-development and growth.

The general public will find it difficult to accept disabled people as equals if people in the helping professions do not. The training programs for people already in the human service fields must focus on the development in professionals of more positive attitudes toward disabled people. Social services professionals are as guilty of negative attitudes as the general public.

---

[1]S. Harasymiw, M. D. Horne, S. C. Lewis, and R. Baron. Teacher and Pupil Disability Attitude Congruency, Paper presented Chicago, Illinois, Annual International Exceptional Children Convention, April 1976.

If the physician, teacher, psychologist, or counselor takes the "he never will be able to make it on his own but we'll try to help" attitude, how can the family or individual have the confidence to go all out and achieve as much as possible? Professionals must help the family of handicapped people to understand and accept, then together all help educate the significant others and, finally, the general public. The employer who believes a handicapped person is an inferior producer will not hire the handicapped or, if he does hire handicapped persons, will not promote to the same levels unless the employer is educated and, in fact, experiences superior performance by handicapped individuals.

In some instances, the fear which normal people experience is really based on the fear that they themselves are not reacting properly. They do not understand what is expected of them. Conversations with disabled people reflect that both the walking person and the paraplegic are disconcerted by the blind person who turns his head away from eye contact so that his ear is the part of the anatomy being addressed. That may help the blind person hear better and therefore understand but disconcerts the seeing person if it is unexpected.

Mentally retarded or deaf people are as disconcerted by the unexpectedness of the epileptic's seizure as the intellectually alert or hearing person. When confronted with a person who suddenly falls down, goes into convulsions, turns blue, and emits strange noises everyone who is unaware the person has epilepsy and unaware of "what to do" is traumatized. Wrong diagnosis — "Oh my god he's dying call an ambulance!" — or right diagnosis wrong treatment dredged up out of the past — "It's an epileptic seizure, put a spoon in his mouth!" or "Don't let him swallow his tongue!" — further intensifies the panic. Communication and education can change this portion of the fear, public education as well as education from the epileptic — "If someone has a seizure just move hard objects out of the way, don't restrain the person having the seizure. The tongue is attached, it can't be swallowed. Sometimes breathing stops during a seizure so the person turns blue. Normal color will resume when breathing resumes. The seizure will be over in a few minutes just stay calm and let the person rest quietly for a little while. If the seizure goes on for ten to fifteen minutes or one seizure follows another and another then call for medical help. Status elipticus requires medical intervention." When a person knows what is expected of him anxiety diminishes. The consumer must play a major role in this type of education but a professionally engineered program of education is required as well.

Stigma

Stigma, written by Erving Goffman[2] in 1963, is subtitled *Notes on the Management of Spoiled Identity.* Goffman says the term stigma refers to an attribute that is deeply discrediting. He analyzes the ways stigmatized individuals feel about themselves and their relationship to others. Clearly, the physically handicapped, mentally retarded, ex-mental patients, and other minority groups must daily confront and be affronted by the image which others reflect back to them.

Goffman says that normals' definition of "good adjustment" on the part of a stigmatized individual requires that this individual cheerfully and unselfconsciously accept himself as essentially the same as normals. At the same time, he voluntarily withholds himself from those situations in which normals would find it difficult to give lip service to their acceptance of him.

Goffman points out that the normal and the stigmatized are not persons but rather perspectives.

Attitudes Relating to the Disability Each Individual Fears Acquiring for Himself and the Conflict between Expressed Attitudes and Feelings

D.O. Hebb (1946) postulates a neurophysiological theory resulting from observations of man's and chimpanzee's spon-

---

[2]E. Goffman, *Stigma: Notes on the Management of Spoiled Identity* (Englewood Cliffs, New Jersey, Prentice Hall, Inc., 1963).

taneous fear of mutilated and unresponsive bodies. He attributes the fear to conflict (primarily of a cerebral nature) resulting from perception of objects that are both familiar (thus compatible) and unfamiliar (thus disruptive).[3] Fear implies that the organism is threatened by some foreign object.

Shonty[4] relates to Lazarus's observation that the "key to whether a situation is appraised as stressful is whether it arouses an anticipation of harm — stress is virtually equivalent to threat."

Charles J. Vander Kolk in *New Outlook for the Blind,* March 1976, measured stress in relation to eleven characteristics. His study indicated that some people experience little stress toward the disabled, while others will psychologically react negatively to nearly any disability. Certain disabilities and characteristics elicited stress more often than others. Subjects were asked to list in order the characteristics they would be most willing to acquire and the ones they would be least willing to acquire. The choices were black, blind, cerebral palsied, diabetic, ex-convict, homosexual, mentally retarded, one arm amputee, one leg amputee, paraplegic, psychotic. Subjects chose being black or diabetic as the characteristics they would be most willing to acquire of the eleven listed, yet they were in the top four in terms of creating high stress.

In this study, cerebral palsy and blindness elicited the most stress. Dr. Vander Kolk used a self-report technique, asking students to list on paper the disability they would be most willing to acquire, then verbalize each choice while being tape recorded. The Psychological Stress Evaluator, an instrument which measures a person's stress by charting voice modulations from a tape recorder, was used to analyze stress. There was a clear discrepancy between the participants' stated preferences and the order found when measuring discomfort with the Psychological Stress Evaluator.[5] In other words their feelings are in con-

---

[3]D. O. Hebb. "On the Nature of Fear," *Psychological Review, 53,* 1946, pp. 259-276.

[4]F. C. Shonty, *The Psychological Aspects of Physical Illness and Disability,* (New York, MacMillan, 1975), pp. 134-135.

[5]C. J. Vander Kolk. "Physiological Measures as a Means of Assessing Reactions to the Disabled," *New Outlook for the Blind,* American Foundation for the Blind, March 1976.

flict with what they believe or *wish* is their belief.

Gottlieb and Siperstein[6] demonstrated that even college students familiar to some extent with mental retardation had significantly more negative attitudes toward severely retarded individuals than toward mildly retarded individuals. It may be that the degree of severity correlates to an increased reluctance to acquire a specific characteristic. Given the choice of acquiring cerebral palsy which affected one finger of one hand or cerebral palsy which affected all parts of the body except one finger, the least desirable would more likely be the more severe limitation. The disability eliciting the most stress may be the one each individual most fears acquiring. The likelihood of acquiring it may be still another factor. Numerous studies indicate blindness is the most feared disability. Since fear of darkness is high and is easily experienced it is understandable that blindness would be most feared. That does not, however, have anything to do with blind people being the most feared. The most feared disabled people would be more apt to be those who offer the greatest threat. This is measured by the desire for social distance between each person.

Attitudes Relating to Social Distance Desired

T. A. Conine's study published in 1969[7] demonstrated that teachers and the general public have similar attitudes toward the disabled.

Jay Gottlieb and Louis Corman of the Research Institute for Educational Problems, found that older respondents, parents of school-age children, and people with no previous contact with a retarded person tended to favor segregation of retarded children in the community and in public school classes.

J. L. Tringo of the University of Connecticut, in his doctoral dissertation (1968), found that a hierarchy of preference of various disability groups existed among rehabilitation profes-

---

[6]J. Gottlieb and G. Siperstein. *American Journal of Mental Deficiency, 80* (4), 1976, pp. 376-381.

[7]T. A. Conine. "Acceptance or Rejection of Disabled Persons by Teachers," *Journal of School Health, 39,* 1969, pp. 278-281.

sionals, similar to that of high school students.[8]

Harasymiw, Horne, and Lewis presented a paper at the National Rehabilitation Association Conference in October 1975[9] demonstrating a hierarchy of societal acceptances for various groups of disabilities by comparing several studies measuring social distance desired, degrees of acceptance from "would accept as an intimate friend" or "would allow to mix with their own group" or "be better off dead." The groups studied were the general population, 1969 and 1974; rehabilitation professionals, 1969; disabled people, 1967; grade-school teachers, 1974; and third-grade students, 1975. The most social distance was desired from (1) the drug addict, (2) the alcoholic, (3) the ex-convict, (4) the mentally ill, (5) the mentally retarded, and (6) the person with tuberculosis.

Harasymiw concludes that this heirarchy is stable across different groups, in accordance with their ability to be productive and to conform to societal values.

Our own experience in developing housing alternatives for three groups of mentally retarded adults, one group of mentally retarded children, and one group of orthopedically handicapped adults each in different communities indicates that Harasymiw's hierarchy of desires for social distance relates to the perceived threat to personal safety or security. The drug addict and alcoholic presents a threat of unpredictable bizzare behavior. There are many commonly held perceptions: If addicts lived in my block they might get my child hooked, rob us for money to buy drugs, or harm or even kill us when they are high. The ex-convict may rob or murder us or influence the children. The mentally ill person could become violent and harm us. The women might take our children or morally corrupt our men. The mentally retarded men might rape our wives and daughters. The person with tuberculosis might infect us and we might become very ill. Most threatening is the possible

---

[8]J. L. Tringo, *The Hierarchy of Preference: A Comparison of Attitudes and Prejudice toward Specific Disability Groups,* (Starrs, University of Connecticut, 1968).

[9]S. J. Harasymiw, M. D. Horne, and S. C. Lewis, *Attitude Congruence of Handicapped and Non-handicapped towards Disability Groups.* Paper presented at National Rehabilitation Association National Conference, Cincinnati, Ohio, October 15, 1975.

loss of life, next bodily harm short of death, and then loss of something of value — a material asset or economic security.

The threat to economic security can help explain the employer's reluctance to hire a handicapped or other minority group person because he will not work hard enough or is unable to produce enough to justify paying him. The employer is also worried, however, that co-workers will not like working with certain kinds of handicapped people and his *good* workers may quit or become rebellious and unproductive. The restaurant owner or maitre d' does not want diners who would make his regular clientele feel uncomfortable. This is demonstrated by an outrageous but very real story of a cerebral palsied man and his wife who were fond of gourmet food and went to a renowned restaurant which they found on arrival was on the second floor accessible only by a staircase. The man let his wife carry his collapsible wheelchair upstairs and he crawled up the stairs — a determined gourmet. The maitre d' greeted them at the top of the stairs with mouth agape and horrified eyes. Seeing the stricken look on the face of the maitre d', the gentleman ascending the stairs said, "It's alright, I can manage." The maitre d' replied, "No, no you can't come in here. It will upset the other guests." (Unspoken was the thought, "And the other guests won't come back and we will lose business.")

The ascending diner insisted and he and his wife were grudgingly seated in a darkened corner. The food was excellent but the service was not. The chef was unaware of this situation and did his usual best. The maitre d' would prefer they did not return and therefore did not shower them with the usual niceties.

In addition to the fear that self and family may be endangered by the behavior of newcomers is the fear expressed by neighbors who find a group of people who are different moving into their block. Those who are different represent a threat to economic security. (If *they* move in property values will go down because *they* are not desirable neighbors. Consequently, my house, which is my major financial asset, will be worth less money because people will not want to move into this neighborhood.)

Identifying Feelings

It is the elimination of the basic fears which reflect threats to personal security that will have the most permanent, long-term, positive effect on integration.

In order to identify the source of negative attitudes regarding integrating mentally retarded people into neighborhoods, we conducted three survey sessions for a total of 63 people in the communities in which two of our facilities were located. Group 1 in the study was a homeowners' association which represented people who lived within less than 10 blocks of a house just purchased as a home for mentally retarded children. This group attended a homeowners' association meeting. Group 2 was composed of women who lived near a small apartment project for retarded women. This group attended a coffee held by mutual friends. Group 3 was both men and women who lived near the same apartment project. They attended a coffee held by mutual friends for the purpose of discussing the residential project.

In Group 1, the most outspoken opponent to the project would not come to the homeowners' association meeting to hear about the program because he felt he "would be sold a bill of goods." In other words, he wished to maintain his negative position without fear of being swayed to a more positive position. (Don't confuse me with facts — I've already made up my mind.)

In Group 2, very few negative feelings were expressed orally; however, the written questionnaires answered and turned in anonymously indicated negative feelings.

In Group 3, the most outspoken critic of the residential apartment building for women would not attend a meeting nor would he fill out a questionnaire on his feelings. He felt it was not right to let mentally retarded women live in the neighborhood. He lived more than 10 blocks away but his mother lived next door to the facility and he was concerned about her safety. He expressed concern about the morals of retarded women and the effect their apartment building would have on the community.

These reactions indicated to us that people who are invited to a meeting may refuse to attend if they feel negatively and can do nothing to change the project. If they are invited by a friend, they might tend to *voice* only positive reactions, especially if they know their hostess is a supporter of the project. It also appears the peer pressure in a community that places high value on programs for handicapped people might keep people from expressing negative feelings even though they are there. Orally, the two groups meeting at a friend's house all said the project was a worthy one; however, when given the opportunity to express their feelings confidentially in a written questionnaire they were clearly less than positive or comfortable. The homeowners association meeting forum lent itself to more open verbalization of fear and opposition.

The 63 people surveyed revealed that approximately one-third of the total group lived within one block of a residential facility and of that 40 percent felt positively about having the facility there, 40 percent were uncertain about the facility and how they felt about it, and 20 percent felt clearly negative. Approximately another one-third lived more than one block and less than five blocks away. In this group the number of positive feelings increased to 73 percent, uncertain decreased to 13 and one-half percent, and negative decreased to 13 percent. The remaining one-third lived more than five blocks away. Their feelings increased to 81 percent positive, negative feelings decreased to 5 percent, and the uncertain held approximately constant at 14 percent. Of all the negative feelings expressed, 80 percent of those individuals lived within five blocks of the facility involved.

Conclusion

These findings demonstrated that resistance to integration increased with proximity. However, since the number of people living in close proximity (less than five blocks away) is numerically limited, potential supporters include everyone who lives *more* than five blocks away. This group would, in most communities, be many times larger than the immediate neighbors.

The Effect Involvement Has on Changing Attitudes

Stefan J. Harasymiw of Northwestern University and Marcia D. Horne of Rhode Island College, Providence, studied teacher attitudes toward retarded children.[10] Those teachers who previously had no experience with handicapped children and were involved in integrated classes for retarded and normal children, with the special assistance of 18 retrained generic specialists, had significantly more positive attitudes as the results of being involved. A control group of teachers who had no experience with an integrated program maintained more negative attitudes. Harasymiw and Horne stated, "The experience of being involved in the project was helpful in contributing to favorable attitudes on the part of the teachers. The experience of working with handicapped children tended to alleviate some of their fears and gave them more confidence in their abilities to handle handicapped children in their classes."

Interestingly, one of the two strongest opponents to the home for mentally retarded children, within three months of the children moving in, became the strongest advocate. Many other groups have reported similar experiences. Once people see, are exposed to, or get involved with the formerly stigmatized group, their negative attitudes and opposition change.

Just as Harasymiw found that teachers' attitudes became more positive as the result of "involvement," so can other attitudes be changed. Involve the general and special public who have negative feelings and if they simply "see" or will permit themselves to be involved, their negative feelings have a great likelihood of becoming positive, as differentness and unfamiliarity becomes familiar and then more compatible and acceptable.

As long as people who are different remain isolated, their differentness is maintained and fear based on unfamiliarity re-

---

[10]S. J. Harasymiw and M. D. Horne. "Integration of Handicapped Children — Its Effect on Teacher Attitudes," *Education, 96* (2), Winter, 1975.

mains.

Goffman's observation that the stigmatized are perspectives not persons, leads us to realize that those perspectives are perpetuated by individuals, by groups, and by the media. To change those perspectives, we must educate persons and groups individually and through the media. This means *especially* educating editors, writers, actors, and producers of all media.

We are only now beginning to see black people and other racial groups as a regular matter on television commercials, programs, and in films. Drug addicts, alcoholics, the mentally ill, the mentally retarded, the blind, and cerebral palsied people are not included routinely in such media exposure. They are either the central character in a story or are not depicted. They are seldom shown in commercials.

The only advertisements the author has ever seen picturing a handicapped person as advocate of a product are for products designed specifically for people with the limitation depicted by the person photographed. Would the interests of the advertiser be served just as well if in group scenes one person was in a wheelchair or carried a white cane or had Down's Syndrome? Could the corporate conscience be served without sacrificing sales? Would the constant exposure of people with those differences enhance the opportunity to create acceptance? Would the depiction of such characteristics with real models encourage larger sales of those products to people who have or are sensitive to the need to familiarize others?

The printed media has learned to be fairly sensitive in reporting about racial minority groups and women by using egalitarian language. Writing about physically handicapped and mentally retarded people still is done with journalistic compassion, which many consumers feel is patronizing, pitying, and perpetuates sympathy rather than understanding and acceptance. Can the local newspaper personnel be educated to express acceptance rather than pity?

In dealing with the uninitiated, can people employed or volunteering in the helping professions and people who possess the stigmatized characteristics and their families assume the role of educator and even therapist? Can we help the uninformed or misinformed overcome their unacceptable behavior — discrimination based on fear of the unfamiliar? Even after a significant effort at education and involvement, can we all realize some people will remain negative and that is their right as long as they do not abuse the civil rights of individuals whom they chose to discriminate against? In the case of physical, mental, and emotional limitations, can we admit that most of us would prefer not to have limitations or experience loss and that we all may, in fact, fear acquiring certain characteristics? How can we be honest and help people recognize their feelings and then provide ways for them to behave consistent with their beliefs?

SECTION III

Where to Start — What to Do

Chapter 9

START BY OPENING THE DOOR

IF we want to gain acceptance for handicapped people, then we must communicate their needs and potentials to the general community. This means focusing attention on them. LeUnes, Christensen, and Wilkerson[1] found tours of facilities for disabled people had a general positive effect in correcting misconceptions regarding mental retardation. The observation of approximately 2,500 college students over eight years were substantiated and documented by the authors. They found that subjects who initially held more negative attitudes changed more in the positive direction than did subjects whose initial attitude was positive. The authors concluded "this was probably due to the fact, as mentioned earlier, that the initial negative attitude group had more room to change in the positive direction since some members of the positive attitude group may have experienced a ceiling effect."

These findings were in general agreement with the results of investigations by Cleland and Chambers (1950) and Kimbrell and Luckey (1964).

Education through the dissemination of information includes a complete willingness on the part of the agencies operating developmental services to have an open door policy.

Policies can be established to protect the clients from disruption of their program during times visitors are touring. The well-intentioned professional who feels clients should not be on "display" and therefore expresses an unwillingness to let people from the community see the programs in operation, creates an aura of mystery and suspicion about what goes on. If the community cannot see handicapped people learning, then

[1]A. LeUnes, L. Christensen, and D. Wilkerson. "Institutional Tour Effects on Attitudes Related to Mental Retardation," *American Journal of Mental Deficiency, 79* (6), pp. 732-735.

obviously, there is something to be hidden. Is it the handicapped person or the way he is being taught?

Focusing attention on disabled people is normal simply because most people like attention. Fashion is created to draw attention to individuals and let them express themselves through their appearance. The object of fashion is to permit the expression of individuality. The individual voluntarily says, "Look at me, I'm different." By contrast, the disabled person is taught to hide his difference. Professionals have become so concerned about teaching the disabled person to look "normal" and diminish his "difference" that they feel the openness required by the community puts the disabled person on display. The professional may be imposing his own negative attitude that disabled people are inferior (see Harasymiw, *Teacher and Pupil Disability Attitude Congruency*).

Anyone who is doing something of which he is ashamed does not want to be on display. However, if one is doing something of which he can be proud, he need not fear the interest and attention of others. Working and learning are activities of which one can be proud. If the professional is proud of his work and would not mind someone coming to watch him, why would he not be willing to let the disabled person show off his ability? The protectiveness of professional staff, in the name of nonexploitation, perpetuates the idea in the mind of both client and public that the client's "state of being" and the activities in the developmental program are not something to be openly viewed.

Many schools, colleges, factories, and work places encourage public visits. Why should there be a difference in the operation of a developmental program? However, the disruption of programs in order to accommodate visitors is unfair to the client. Therefore, tours which permit the uninterrupted operation of programs should be the goal of agencies interested in being open about their activities and thereby educating the community.

Audio-visual presentations are good, but with the current level of sophistication regarding the use and misuse of film and tape to create an illusion, on-site visits communicate with a greater degree of effectiveness. There is no substitute for "I saw it with my own eyes."

The policy of openness usually results initially in many on-site visits, followed by a leveling off of visits and eventually the willingness to accept audio-visual presentations at meetings because it is so difficult to get all the members of organizations to meet somewhere other than their usual place.

Although rehabilitation is not new, large portions of the rehabilitation process have been conducted under wraps. For those outside the field of rehabilitation, the unveiling of the process by which disabilities are eliminated or compensated for creates a sense of wonder and appreciation. When this sense of wonder and appreciation is expressed by a respected member of the community, who has seen with his own eyes, the impact is substantial.

When we began to interest the influential people in our community in the needs of handicapped people, they were willing to help. Months later when one of our luncheon meetings was held in our workshop, the reality of all we had been discussing theoretically struck home. The workshop was sizeable, even substantially handicapped clients were working in a businesslike way on a variety of complicated tasks. Specific individuals who were treated with tolerance in the community were working competently at a variety of tasks. This revelation turned interest into commitment for several people.

The staff person in charge of community education cannot do an effective job if the rest of the professional staff does not understand the real value of changing the environment and the need to educate as part of the change process.

Arrangements for on-site visits might be made by the community education staff person. He may even give a brief background description of the agency and the programs. The director of the program or another staff person in that program might explain the activities.

This insures that the latest program changes are incorporated into the "tour" and it permits the spokesman to express his own perceptions. It is most ideal if people have the opportunity to talk with several staff members and a client. Visitors are impressed with the relative normalcy of the special education classroom, the workshop, and the residence. They are also impressed by signs of either opulence or frugality.

If, during a visit, everything is not going smoothly, a fight breaks out or an accident occurs, it just confirms the reality of the program — that it is not a place where miracles occur smoothly and with regularity. It is a place where staff people trained in their jobs work very hard to achieve a goal. If the goal is toilet training Johnny, and Johnny is obviously having none of it at the moment, several things are communicated:

1. People work in rehabilitation as a profession.
2. They are human.
3. They are skilled.
4. The person being rehabilitated is human.
5. He may disagree with the staff person.
6. He may cooperate with the staff person.
7. Some people want to learn.
8. Some people do not want to learn.

Most lay people have great respect for the work done by professionals in rehabilitation. They sometimes even credit them with superhuman qualities. Everyone likes to be admired for his accomplishments, but it is quite tiring living up to the belief that one is superhuman. Perhaps we should put more emphasis on the relative magnificence of the disabled person's achievements and admit that even here, the teacher learns much from his student — it is a teaching relationship of equals. Equality in the community must be preceded by equality in the place of learning.

Chapter 10

ENCOURAGE VOLUNTEERS

PAUL, Wiegerink, and Neufeld[1] point out –

Professionals in the field of special education and rehabilitation frequently feel that even if public citizens wish to become involved in service delivery as volunteers, training them takes more time than it's worth. To the extent that these attitudes exist, one can understand the impulse of professionals to undertake program development and service delivery without involving parents or the general public.

If professionals were adequately serving the needs of handicapped persons without help from parents and other public citizens, we could accept their independence. Since confusion seems to reign in the human service network and since we continue to be faced with many unmet needs, a strong case can be made for the development of sound linkages with the general public.

Areas of support that can be provided by the general public range from direct service and individual and program monitoring, to participation on boards and political lobbying. In each of these areas, professionals should assume responsibility for recruitment, organization, and training.

In the area of direct service, it is clear that in the foreseeable future there will not be sufficient public resources to provide the kind of staff to client ratios that are necessary to adequately serve the needs of disabled persons. At the same time, the interest of parents, the general population, and their potential for providing service has not been realized.

In Nebraska, a program of "live-in friend" involves a citizen advocate sharing an apartment with a retarded person who has been discharged from a residential institution. The occupations of "live-in friends" are benefactors (Heber and Dever, 1970) and teachers for their roommate in money management, shopping, use of public transportation, cooking,

---

[1]D. J. Stedman, *Advocacy: A Role for Developmental Disabilities Councils,* monograph edited by J. L. Paul, R. Wiegerink, and G. R. Neufeld, 1974, pp. 24-25.

self-medication, use of telephones, and leisure time activities. It has been reported that the program is effective and economical.

Volunteerism has taken some harsh criticism by the women's liberation movement. The critics maintain that women should be paid for the work they now do as volunteers, and in fact have placed such high value on "paid work" that many women give up satisfying volunteer and family activities to pursue a career. Frequently, the career is a $2.00-an-hour job as a saleslady or clerk which may or may not help the individual in her search for self-actualization.

At the same time, men who feel their paid employment does not offer adequate opportunities for self-fulfillment are making their time available for volunteer activities that are meaningful to them.

It may take feminists time to re-examine the validity of improving self-worth and self-fulfillment only through paid employment; in the meantime, scores of women still welcome the opportunity to be needed.

Volunteer activities should be varied enough in scope and flexible enough in design to enhance the opportunity for growth in each individual whether volunteer or client.

The voluntary aspect of life in our society provides opportunities for all citizens to volunteer their time and talents in helping disabled people, so that each handicapped person can choose where and how he lives. The disabled person who develops abilities which enable him to cope with life may then also choose to help his fellow man.

A physically handicapped woman learned literary and painting skills and became both an artist and poet. She now shares her ability to cope through drawings and poems. Others who are not necessarily physically disabled, but who do have difficulty coping with everyday challenges, benefit from her experience and talent when they buy her books.

The process of man helping man is circular. Enabling one person to meet his own needs by letting that person help another could be the goal of a program to incorporate volunteers into the process of social change necessary to meet the needs of handicapped people. Help one, help another, and all benefit.

Whether the organized body of volunteers consists of all women, both men and women of all ages, or just young people, the basic organizational mechanism is the same. Marlene Wilson has written "The Effective Management of Volunteer Programs" which contains the elements of any good management process.

1. Plan by establishing goals and objectives.
2. Organize
   by planning what needs to be done
   by designing specific jobs.
3. Staff
   by recruiting
   by interviewing
   by placing volunteers
   by training volunteers.
4. Direct
   by supervising.
5. Control
   by evaluating job value and volunteer performance.

This process, of course, is ongoing. The planning, organizing, directing, and controlling process continues as initial goals are achieved or modified and new goals based on changing needs and availability of resources are established.

Step No. 1

In order to develop the volunteers who are already involved in helping the agency into a manageable resource which responds to direction, the following evaluation should be made.

I. In what areas can you use volunteer assistance?
   A. Children's direct service programs
   B. Adults' direct service programs
   C. Community education
   D. Clerical assistance
   E. Running special events
   F. Fund raising

G. Operating a shop.
   1. As an outlet for goods made by handicapped people
   2. As a retail training ground for clients
   3. As a source of additional income

II. How many volunteers do you have in each area?
   A. Is that enough?
   B. In what area can you use more help?

Step No. 2

Assign an administrative staff member to work with the volunteers. Maximizing the effectiveness of volunteer resources requires management.

Step No. 3

Get Board approval to structure a mechanism for developing a stronger organization in which volunteers can function. Determine whether volunteers should have a structured organization of their own to relate to the policy-making board or relate to the staff.

Organizing a Formal Volunteer Organization

Step No. 1

Select a small committee (5 to 10) members from existing volunteers to determine and select a volunteer governing board.

Step No. 2

Identify what the agency needs for the volunteer governing board, e.g. more help in the classrooms, more money, better communication with the community.

Step No. 3

Determine whether a separate corporation termed "the Auxiliary," "the Volunteer League," etc., or just a separate organization within the existing corporation best meets the agency needs.

Step No. 4

Have the president or chairperson of the volunteer league sit on the board of directors of the agency. The first year the staff and board might recommend who would be the best candidate for president of the volunteer league (perhaps a current board member), but the bylaws of the new organization must permit the members of the volunteer league to elect their own governing board and the board choose their own leaders or officers each year. The group will not function at maximum effectiveness unless the individuals feel that they have chosen their own leadership.

Step No. 5

Have a series of organizational coffees at the homes of prominent leaders in the community featuring the following:

1. An audio-visual description of the agency's purpose, programs, clients, and staff, presented by a well-informed, articulate staff member.
2. Budgetary information — Be prepared to answer questions regarding sources of income, expenses, per capita income, per capita costs, use of voluntary contributions, why you need voluntary contributions.
3. How volunteers can help.
4. How the community can help.

ORGANIZATIONAL STRUCTURE
FOR VOLUNTEER LEAGUE, AUXILIARY, WOMEN'S BOARD, ETC.

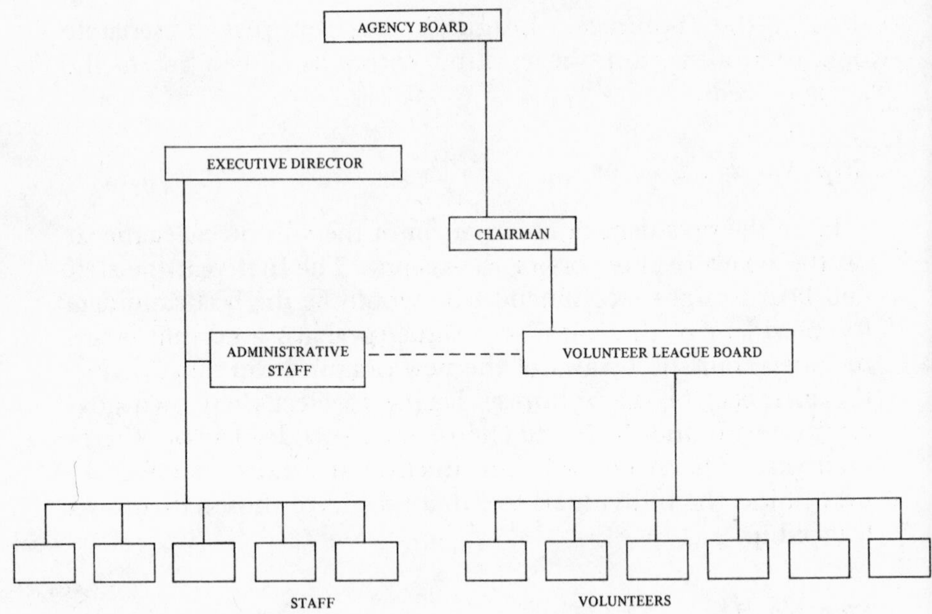

RAY GRAHAM ASSOCIATION FOR THE HANDICAPPED

Volunteer League

ADDRESS & TOWN	PHONE NO.	Indicate Area of Interest BENEFITS	SHOP	CENTER	SCHOOL	SWIMMING	INFANT PROGRAM	OFFICE	TOURS	COFFEES

RAY GRAHAM ASSOCIATION FOR THE HANDICAPPED

515 Factory Rd., Addison 60101 543-2440

Bonaparte School Volunteer Sheet

Name:____
(Last) (First) (Husband)

Address: ________________________________Phone:________
(Street) (City) (Zip)

Child in program Yes____ No____

Day(s) of week I can come: Mon. Tues. Wed. Thurs. Fri. (Please circle)
School hours are 9:00 a.m. to 2:00 p.m.

Hours I can volunteer are ______ to ______

I have no preference as to room assignment Yes____ No____

I prefer to work with children age
3 - 8_____
9 - 12_____
16 and up_____

I prefer to work with teacher (name) ______________________

or in room (name)______________________

I can help with swimming program Yes____ No____
I can help with the bowling program Yes____ No____

Please return to Bonaparte School
300 E. Cole
Wheaton, Ill. 60187
Phone: 665-4560

Office Use Only

Room Assignment_____
Day(s)________
Hours________
R.________

Sunshine Gift Shop Volunteer Sheet

NAME ____
(Last) (First) (Husband)

ADDRESS ______________________________________ PHONE__________
(Street) (Town) (Zip)

Days and hours I can volunteer: (Please check days and fill in hours.)

__Monday	Hrs.__to__	__Thursday	Hrs.__to__
__Tuesday	Hrs.__to__	__Friday	Hrs.__to__
__Wednesday	Hrs.__to__	__Saturday	Hrs.__to__

Office Use Only
DATE________ ASSIGNMENT: Day________Hours______________

Special Events Volunteer Sheet

NAME ____
(Last) (First) (Husband)

ADDRESS ______________________________________ PHONE__________
(Street) (Town) (Zip)

I would be willing to:	*Days and hours available*
____ Sell tickets.	________ FROM __ TO __
____ Recruit volunteers	________ FROM __ TO__
____ Do clerical work.	________ FROM __ TO __
____ Solicit ads.	________ FROM __ TO __
____ Act as a hostess.	________ FROM __ TO __

____ Help with miscellaneous tasks such as baking, organizing, handling reservations, distributing tickets, etc.

Those people who are extroverts might enjoy conducting tours of the programs, making speeches, recruiting other volunteers, and chairing committees. Introverted personalities can play just as vital a role working in an art shop, selling gift items, quietly explaining the needs and programs of the agency and the people it services, doing clerical work of a nonconfidential nature, manning an information booth at an exposition or fair, and having neighbors in for coffee to learn what is happening in rehabilitation in your town.

Maintaining the delicate balance of developing volunteers as a resource to meet the needs of people with problems (your agency's goals) and providing an opportunity for volunteers to meet their own needs and grow as individuals is a highly complicated task.

John M. Pfiffner, in the book *Administrative Organization,* joins his perception with Chris Argyris, author of *Personality and Organization,* to explain how each person arrives at his own individual integration of personal needs.

Since the management of human resources requires understanding human personality needs, it would be appropriate to discuss Argyris's ideas and their particular relevance to the use of volunteers. Volunteer activity does not meet the individual's economic need, it relates almost totally to personality need.

Personality Characteristics

Argyris has prepared an excellent summary of this problem in *Personality and Organization.*[2] The ideas expressed in the following paragraphs are taken largely from that source and suggest that personalities are similar in the following respects:

1. Personality must be viewed as a system of organizing drives and predispositions. The parts, such as honesty, loyalty, and initiative, cannot be taken out of the system and viewed independently.

2. The parts of the personality stick together because each part uses one or more other parts in order to exist. This occurs

---

[2]C. Argyris, *Personality and Organization* (New York: Harper and Row, 1957), Chapter 2.

both internally and externally. Internally, a balance exists when the parts of the personality are in equilibrium with each other; externally, the balance occurs when the personality as a whole is in equilibrium with the outside environment.

3. The personality manifests energy. In Argyris's view, the expression of this energy has significance to the administrator for these reasons:

> Everyone has such energy.
> This energy is indestructible.
> The extent to which this energy is manifested depends on the individual's attitudes at any particular time.
> If the expression of this energy is blocked, the individual will seek its expression in some other way.
> If the expression of the energy is channelled in an unsatisfactory way, there will be an attempt to express it elsewhere.[3]

4. The energy of the personality comes from the individual's need system. The extent to which energy is expressed in any one direction depends on the intensity of the need and the degree to which satisfaction is achieved.

5. The personality has abilities, of which three types may be noted. These are (a) the knowing (cognitive) abilities, (b) the doing (motor) abilities, and (c) the feeling abilities.

6. Personalities have common mechanisms for dealing with threats. One of these is to change one's self in a fashion necessary to eliminate the threat. The other is to deny or distort that which is threatening.

7. As the individual matures, he not only acquires more parts, i.e. more needs and abilities, but he also deepens many of them. These new additions must be so arranged in the total personality system as not to destroy its essential balance.

Individual Maturation

The concept of individual maturation seems a particularly important one. Here is a growth process which is common to

[3]Argyris, p. 25.

all people but whose rate and character of development differs from individual to individual. It is also worth noting that in the maturation process, there is conveyed a real sense of a dynamic organism which is growing and changing, reacting to new stimuli, and creating new equilibrium patterns. As a consequence, it is not surprising that Argyris has accorded this concept very considerable significance in his theory of organization behavior.

Dimensions

Argyris suggests that there are certain dimensions to this maturation process, which apply generally in the American culture. We all start at zero on the scale of each of these dimensions and reach varying points along the scale in the process of growth and development. The following dimensions were identified by Argyris:

> The development from a start of dependence upon others as infants to a state of relative independence as adults.
>
> The development from a state of passivity as infants to a state of increasing activity as adults.
>
> The development from behavior capabilities in only a few ways as an infant to behavior capabilities in many ways as an adult.
>
> The development from erratic, casual, shallow, quickly dropped interests as an infant to deeper interests as an adult.
>
> The development from short time perspective (i.e. the present largely determines behavior) as an infant to a much longer time perspective as an adult (i.e. where the behavior is more affected by the past and the future).
>
> The development from a subordinate position in the family and society as an infant to a position equal to one's peers or higher than them.
>
> The development from a lack of awareness of one's self as an infant to an awareness and control over one's self as an adult.[4]

The first priority then, in establishing a volunteer program,

[4]Argyris, p. 50.

is to meet the needs of disabled people by developing opportunities for many people to offer their time and resources so that they may meet their own needs for self-fulfillment and social acceptance.

It is imperative that a structure be provided within which volunteers can work. More than once enthusiastic volunteerism has developed into activities which are not consistent with programmatic goals. Meeting the needs of the volunteers replaced meeting the needs of the program and the people that it serves.

Our agency volunteers at one time operated a thrift shop — accepting second-hand clothes as donations and selling them in a small store. When geographical boundaries for service areas were redistributed, the store was outside our agency's cachement area. Since the retail operation had value, we sold it to the agency serving that area.

The volunteer board wanted to start another store but found rentals in our area were much higher. This was in the early stages of our community education programs. Our staff felt too many negative attitudes were perpetuated by the agency operating a store which sold cast-off clothes. People frequently gave clothes and household items that were barely usable. The philosophy of the giver was usually, "Well, the family and I can't use it anymore, but I'll bet that handicapped group would appreciate it." The concept of castoffs and second-rate had become associated with handicapped. Even worse, "It's good enough for those poor souls being so wretched they'll appreciate anything," was the well-intentioned but negative thought behind the gift.

We, therefore, suggested to our volunteers, that a shop which emphasized the positive aspects of rehabilitation and the abilities of disabled people, rather than pity, would be more consistent with our goal of creating an atmosphere of understanding and awareness for the needs and abilities of handicapped people.

A gift shop selling handmade art and craft items made by both handicapped and nonhandicapped craftsmen was chosen to be the project. The Sunshine Shop's official opening was graced by the governor's wife and over 100 volunteers. An artistically talented local woman, with experience in retail sales and business, manages the shop. She contacts the craftsmen, takes the merchandise on consignment, and teaches homebound handicapped people how to make items which would be saleable in the store.

As time passed the store was also used as a retail training program. The volunteers were used as sales help in the shop. The shop was open six days a week from 9:30 to 5:30. It became apparent that volunteers were not available all the times regular shops were open. The volunteers suggested closing the shop when they were not available. Since the messages we were trying to convey were "handicapped people are good workers," "the Ray Graham Association workshops are like any other business," "their prices are competitive and they meet delivery dates;" closing the shop one day during the week meant losing a day's training for the handicapped clients, closing the shop on Saturday meant losing business.

We, therefore, decided the manager would be in the shop three full days a week to supervise training and out two days a week securing merchandise and making home visits. The other three days the shop was to be staffed by volunteers and a client since hiring a second person would use up all profits and create a deficit.

The role of the volunteers was defined — the staff was responsible for the operation of the shop and the volunteers provided auxiliary help which enabled the manager to visit homebound people. Using volunteers only three days a week cut down the recruiting and scheduling burden. Distinguishing programmatic goals, community education goals, and fundraising goals helped establish priorities.

The first reason for the operation of the shop was to provide an outlet for handcrafted items made by handicapped craftsmen. In order to carry a full inventory and simultaneously communicate that these items were first-rate quality and indistinguishable from items made by nondisabled people, articles were also accepted on the same basis from nonhandicapped craftsmen, two-thirds of the sale price went to the craftsman and one-third to the shop for operating costs.

The second reason for the existence of the shop was to provide retail training experience for workshop clients.

The third reason for the existence of the shop was to relate to the general public certain information:

1. Handicapped people can produce desirable goods.
2. Handicapped people can work in retail stores.
3. A not-for-profit agency providing developmental services can function in a businesslike way.
4. Profits from the shop were used to teach severely handicapped homebound people and encourage them to venture into the mainstream of life.

The volunteers' role included the following:

1. To augment, but not replace, the manager in the shop.
2. To stretch the money available from the operation of the shop to cover the cost of training homebound people and provide retail training and experience for others.
3. To act as communicators for the agency regarding its programs and the capacities of disabled people.

In order to insure that organizational goals are achieved, policy regarding the utilization of volunteers must be adopted. Volunteers can be a tremendously valuable resource; conservation and development of that resource requires thought and continued attention.

The volunteer coordinator or, if there is only one staff member, the community education coordinator needs to be able to match the talents of people in the community with the needs of handicapped people and the goals of the agency. Volunteers cannot always articulate what they do best. The volunteer coordinator must have a personnel director's insight into the most effective use of the human resources available. The difference, of course, is that the volunteer is not paid in money. The community education coordinator or volunteer coordinator must see that the compensation given to each volunteer is in the medium of exchange which is valued by that individual. Sometimes the volunteer job itself is the reward. Just seeing an individual child's progress is adequate compensation. For others, public or peer recognition of their level of achievement is needed. In other words, being named "Legislative

Chairman," "Volunteer Chairman," "Benefit Chairman," or "Membership Drive Chairman" is the reward for effective leadership. This type of recognition carries with it additional responsibilities which only true leaders value. Volunteers who have been effective, but do not want or value additional responsibility, can be recognized with just a simple "thank you" from the teacher or staff person they have been helping. Some people give so much of themselves, even all those warm *thank yous* seem inadequate; then an award for outstanding achievement is appropriate.

Once the truly outstanding volunteer has been publicly awarded every honor the agency has to bestow and still keeps on working, he might be included as a judge in the selection process for other awards.

J. Donald Philips, president of Hillsdale College, Hillsdale, Michigan, drew up ten points which clearly express the "Volunteer Viewpoint."

VOLUNTEER VIEWPOINT[5]

If you want my loyalty, interests, and best efforts, remember that . . .

1. I need a SENSE OF BELONGING, a feeling that I am honestly needed for my total self, not just for my hands, nor because I take orders well.
2. I need to have a sense of sharing in planning our objectives. My need will be satisfied only when I feel that my ideas have had a fair hearing.
3. I need to feel that the goals and objectives arrived at are within reach and that they make sense to me.
4. I need to feel that what I'm doing has real purpose or contributes to human welfare — that its value extends even beyond my personal gain, or hours.
5. I need to share in making the rules by which, together, we shall live and work toward our goals.
6. I need to know in some clear detail just what is expected of me — not only my detailed task but where I have

[5]J. D. Philips, President of Hillsdale College, Hillsdale, Michigan. Adapted from *Volunteers Today: Finding, Training, and Working with Them,* by H. H. Naylor.

opportunity to make personal and final decisions.

7. I need to have some responsibilities that challenge, that are within range of my abilities and interest, and that contribute toward reaching my assigned goal, and that cover all goals.
8. I need to see that progress is being made toward the goals we have set.
9. I need to be kept informed. What I'm not up on, I may be down on. (Keeping me informed is one way to give me status as an individual.)
10. I need to have confidence in my superiors — confidence based upon assurance of consistent fair treatment, or recognition when it is due, and trust that loyalty will bring increased security.

Conclusion

The effective human service organization should be able to recognize that paid staff, volunteer staff, clients, and the general public all have a great deal to give to each other and to learn from each other. If the organization is truly human service oriented, it can help both obviously disabled and the needful enhance their own development through mutual giving. The disabled person teaches more by simply being than the non-disabled.

One particularly effective volunteer turned professional, upon being commended for significant achievements in helping handicapped people, said, "I really think one little mentally retarded girl who needed services that weren't there and therefore started me reaching out to find others to help solve the problem is the true source for significant achievement. Her need helped me grow. My growth helped others, but it was Vicky's very existence which inspired growth in a number of the lives that touched hers and they in turn touched many. Her need was in reality a gift to others of opportunity for learning, growth and thanksgiving. Vicky has given more by her being than any of us have given by helping. Being needed makes my life meaningful. I treasure having something worthy of giving."

SAMPLE VOLUNTEER SERVICES POLICY

The volunteer services program is an organized and carefully supervised activity in which the varied skills of unpaid personnel are utilized to support and supplement the efforts of paid agency staff.

Standards

Volunteer participation is open to persons of both sexes; of all races, creeds, and national origins; and at appropriate ages and varying levels of ability. (We, of course, do not exclude disabled people as volunteers.)

Volunteer participation complies with state laws, such as those relating to labor and insurance.

Volunteer services are available to all clients, regardless of age, ability, or handicaps.

The volunteer coordinator is responsible for the recruitment of volunteers.

The volunteer coordinator has education or experience in the administration of volunteer services.

Each program director defines the number and type of volunteers needed. Volunteers assigned to direct service programs are trained and work under the direction of the professional staff in each program. The volunteer coordinator works with the professional staff to see that accurate records are kept concerning the volunteer's name, address, age, family status, special talents, and availability in terms of hours, as well as the number of hours worked. Indirect service volunteers are trained by and work under the direction of the volunteer coordinator.

Volunteers' names and addresses are regularly incorporated into the mailing list and become part of the constituency of the agency.

The volunteer coordinator has the same relationship to volunteers as a personnel officer has to paid employees.

Recognition is given annually to all volunteers for their assistance at a special event under the direction of the director of development. Special recognition is given to volunteers who have made outstanding contributions to improving the quality of life for handicapped people. The volunteers designated for special recognition are nominated by the professional staff in each area of participation.

A volunteer services advisory committee, composed of representatives from the agency, the clients, and the community, plans, reviews, and recommends improvements in the volunteer program.

Committee Members

1. Agency Board President
2. Agency Executive Director
3. Volunteer League Board President
4. Director of Development
5. Community Education Coordinator
6. Director of Children's Services
7. Representative of Adult Services
8. Manager of Sunshine Shop
9. Director of Recreational Program
10. President of Youth Group
11. Volunteer League recruiter and scheduler
12. Disabled member of the community not on Board
13. Both a male and a female client in adult programs
14. All major Volunteer Chairmen

Chapter 11

TELLING YOUR STORY

Who are you?
What do you do?
Why do you do it?
Where do you do it?
How do you do it?

WHY do you want to tell your story? Is it to communicate the existence of your services to people who need them? Do you want to gain community support for the people that you serve and for the services your organization provides? Because you are an organization located in and supported by the community, do you feel you have a responsibility to be accountable to the community? Do you think higher visibility of the services provided by your organization would more effectively cause people in need of your services to seek them?

When should you tell your story? Once a year? Once a month? Only when asked? Whenever possible, as often as possible? Continually?

What and to whom do you want to communicate? Is it only to handicapped people and their families? Should other people working in allied social and health fields keep informed about what you are doing on a regularly updated basis? Does the general public need to know anything about handicapped people, their needs, their rights, their potential?

How are "they" going to find out about "you?" Who is going to tell them? Are you going to send letters? If so, to whom about what? Should you have a newsletter? Do you need a brochure describing your services? Do you need an annual report with information about services, budget, staff, directors, accomplishments, problems, needs, new plans? Would a film or audio-visual presentation more effectively describe what you want to communicate to some audiences? Is there a need for both written materials and audio-visual materials? Should you know how to deal with mass media?

Following chapters will outline five links in a communication network and the how of communicating. You must decide what, who, and when.

Chapter 12

LINK #1: ESTABLISHING A COMMUNICATION NETWORK — THE CONSTITUENCY

C. D. Browne in "Communication Means Understanding" defines communication as "the process of transmitting ideas or thoughts from one person to another, or within a single person for the purpose of creating understanding in the thinking of the person receiving the communication."[1]

J. K. Pierce in *Symbols, Signals and Noise: The Nature and Process of Communication* says, "In the broadest sense, the aim and outcome of communication is the resolution of uncertainty."[2] It is also "the means of obtaining action from others or from things. It is manifested in many ways — as influence, as authority, or as information flowing through networks of communication channels."

The action required to create an accepting environment in the community begins with the establishment of a communication network.

According to Johnson, Kast, and Rosenzweig in "Systems, Theory and Management" "communication . . . is a system involving a sender and a receiver with implications of feedback control."[3]

Scott and Mitchell in *Organization Theory*[4] say, "An administrative model of communication should contain:

1. Sources to generate information and receivers to assimilate

---

[1]C. G. Browne, "Communication Means Understanding," in K. Davis and W. G. Scott, *Readings in Human Relations* (New York, McGraw-Hill, 1959), p. 331.

[2]J. K. Pierce, *Symbols, Signals and Noise: The Nature and Process of Communication.* (New York, Harper and Row, 1961), p. 79.

[3]R. A. Johnson, F. E. Kast, and J. E. Rosenzweig. "Systems, Theory and Management," *Management Science,* January 1964, p. 380.

[4]W. G. Scott and T. R. Mitchell, *Organization Theory: A Structural and Behavioral Analysis,* rev. ed. (Homewood, Illinois, Richard D. Irwin, Inc., 1976).

it.

2. Vehicles to convey information.
3. A channel."

They see stages of communication development within an organization moving from handicraft, to mechanization, and then to automation as the systems grow.

Most important, Scott and Mitchell say human acceptance of information is affected by the receivers' perception of reality, whether or not there is ambiguity, the credibility of the sender, and whether the information is relevant to the receiver.

Katz and Kahn in "The Social Psychology of Organizations" say human organizations are informational as well as energic systems. They maintain that communication is the essence of a social system or an organization, that more communication is not equivalent to better communication, and that quality is more important than quantity.

To move from an unorganized to an organized state requires establishing and limiting channels of communication. Each subsystem will respond to the same information in different ways and each will seek out particular information to meet its needs. Messages emanating in one part of any organization need translation if they are to be effective in other parts.

The first link in the chain of communication must be the people who have already indicated some interest in handicapped people and the agency's activities. Recognition of a constituency and the establishment of the means of communicating with that group is the first step in establishing a network.

Person to person communication is, of course, the most effective because it allows for discourse and feedback from both sides. This interchange minimizes distortions or misconceptions.

One to one conversations, meetings of small groups of people, and meetings of large groups of people allow for person to person communication. An organization which has an open-ended membership permits the regular exploration of subjects of mutual interest. It allows for the establishment of regular meetings or programs with speakers, panels, and an audience.

Permanently recording the names and addresses of people who attend meetings or indicate their interest in other ways and incorporating those names into a mailing list seems too obvious even to mention, yet many groups who attract an audience through the mass media or by invitation do not take the trouble to have a guest log at every gathering so they may know exactly who is responding and continue to communicate with interested parties.

The establishment and record keeping of a constituency should be an automatic process whereby people who call for information, attend meetings, volunteer their time, contribute their money, or in any way indicate their interest have their names incorporated into a mailing list. The more people are aware of what is happening, the more education takes place.

This constituency will be a link in the communication chain only if they are notified of meetings, needs, and occurrences through mailings of letters, postcards, newsletters, or perhaps even a small magazine. The cost of communicating with 5,000 is very little more than the cost of communicating with 1,000. The major portion of printing costs is borne in the initial 100 pieces; the per unit cost after that declines rapidly. The use of bulk mail postage rates for nonprofit organizations is also relatively low. An automatic addressing system is a necessity.

"Why didn't you let me know? I could have helped." is the situation we are trying to avoid. Response, input, and participation are the result of outward communication.

Special mailings on special subjects to specific audiences is one means of reaching people. A newsletter once a month or six times a year is an effective means of communicating a substantial amount of information on a variety of subjects, and cuts down the postage of numerous mailings.

All materials sent to a constituency should be simply and interestingly written and, of course, reproduced with maximum clarity. The cost of professionally printing a newsletter is usually well-worth the investment because the type is clearly readable and the amount of information compressed into four printed pages would take twelve pages of mimeographed copy.

The savings in paper and postage only can many times pay for the printing cost.

One of the messages we are always trying to express about handicapped people is that they have abilities as well as disabilities. It is therefore especially important that all written material stress the "able" rather than "disabled" or ineffective. Both content design and method must be chosen with care. Poorly duplicated materials with staples falling out clearly say, "No wonder you can't read it; it's from the handicapped people."

Chapter 13

LINK #2: SPEAKERS' BUREAU AND COMMUNICATING THROUGH AUDIO-VISUAL PRESENTATIONS

CONTINUING with the concept of person to person communication, the inception of a speakers' bureau, featuring both audio-visual presentations and dynamic speakers, is another opportunity for both discourse and feedback with the community

All directors of rehabilitation programs are not dynamic speakers. The goal of a speakers' bureau is to communicate effectively with the community using the best resources available. The speakers should be chosen by their ability to express the need and catalyze a response. The speakers may be professionals in the agency, board members, volunteers, or the community education staff itself.

Many an audience has nodded politely through a dissertation of which they understood every fifth word. This type of speech is impressive but not effective.

Academic expressionism is appropriate and effective at a professional conference where the language is familiar to other members of the cult. However, translations and interpretations are required for people outside the cult — in other words, for the other 99 percent of the population.

Academicians and many professionals in the field of rehabilitation pride themselves on being able to discuss what appears to be nuances to those uneducated in the field but are, in fact, important philosophical and technical differences. Therefore, the translation of technical data into everyday language requires the loss of some precision. It is rather like translating an idiom from one language to another. The precise explanation frequently renders the expression impotent and leaves the audience apathetic, whereas the substitution of another idiom with a similar but not exactly the same meaning communicates the point.

Slide presentations with a synchronized tape or live accompaniment are inexpensive to produce and can be constantly updated with minimum cost.

Simple words expressing philosophical approaches and general procedures accompanied by lots of pictures delivered by an informed and interesting speaker are the ideal. The value of good audio-visual materials cannot be underestimated. Trite and true is the saying "One picture is worth 1,000 words." Slides or film of program activities are second only to an on-site visit or tour of the programs. Providing speakers is actually a service to many clubs and organizations who are earnestly seeking both interesting programs and civic projects to support. In fact, our "speakers" program alone has covered the cost of our total community education program staff and materials, by generating gifts from local clubs and organizations as the result of presentations and speeches.

Motion pictures, however, can present a series of ideas and emotions in rapid succession. The pictures on the screen follow each other in an artistic pattern. They create an emotional effect which is the objective of any fine art. The social influence of mass distributed motion pictures cannot be understated.[1]

The filmmaker can use light and shade, shape, size, and angle to synchronize, detail, and assign a purpose and cohesion to the screen image. How the images are chosen and in what sequence they are shown creates the design, and the emotional effects they create are the components which elevate film making to art.

The filmmaker has six elements at his disposal: image, movement, time, space, color, and sound.

The painter expresses himself through color and form. The musical composer uses a succession of sounds in varying relationships and intensities. The writer uses words selected and arranged to communicate facts, feelings, and ideas.

The filmmaker has the raw materials of all three mediums

[1]A. Knight, *The Liveliest Art* (New York, New American Library, 1971).

with which to express and communicate. This gives motion pictures a special quality and maximizes the potential for communicating images and ideas and evoking feelings.

The importance of lighting is emphasized by Lew Jacobs[2] who says that "without illumination of some sort, the motion picture camera could not reproduce the subject's image on film. It is light which enables the camera lens to transmit an image of what is before it into a photographic reproduction. Thus, light and visual composition are interlocked.

Only on-site visits to programs can compete with a sound, color motion picture for effectiveness in communicating the what, how, who, where, and why of developmental programs for handicapped people.

The new color Super 8 mm™ film is less expensive to produce and process but requires the purchase of a Super 8 projector to show it. If target audiences for the film are relatively small, this is a most effective and cost efficient means of producing a film.

In many instances, an agency should expect to reproduce a film of its services at least every year or two because of the many changes which take place within the program. The here and now has very high value in communicating accurately and creating a sense of community awareness.

It is expensive to produce a 16 mm film but it is generally more adaptable to showing to any size audience. The production process of a 16 mm is a great deal more complicated than that of a Super 8, but if the agency is dealing with a large number of different-sized audiences, the 16 mm film might be a first choice.

Eastman Kodak has produced a splendid piece of informational literature on making a movie with Super 8 film, called "Movies With a Purpose." The cost of producing a ten minute Super 8 film is approximately $200.00 plus the cost of the projector needed to show the film. However, 16 mm projectors are readily available to most groups who represent a potential audience. A 16 mm, eight minute film professionally produced would cost approximately $8,000, or $1,000 a minute. We pro-

---

[2]L. Jacobs, *The Movies as Medium* (Garden City, New York, 1970).

duced our own 16 mm film using donated film, processing, recording, and soundtrack. The cost was approximately $400.00

The first step in filmmaking is the same as for any audio-visual presentation — determine what is to be communicated and what visual interpretation will be used to tell the story.

After a script is written, each visual idea can be drawn on a simple set of cards or simply noted in the margin of the script.

Our film incorporated sixty different elements which were shots of specific ideas and activities.

Since we felt there were many negative and erroneous impressions regarding disabled people, we chose color film to create a realistic yet cheerful, positive feeling. The same effect is possible using black and white film, but it requires a much higher degree of sophistication in filming to achieve.

The atmosphere we wished to create was natural, real, and positive. We, therefore, used only natural lighting. Some scenes were then effectively in silhouette, but one scene was too dark!

Using an elderly borrowed camera, we arranged a shooting schedule with each program site. We sent letters home with each client explaining we were making a movie of the services provided by the agency and requesting parents to let us know if they did not want their child or family member photographed. We already had photo releases on 95 percent of the people in the program but wanted to make certain that the families of those 95 percent were comfortable with the idea of having their relative featured in a film. At the time we shot each scene, we asked the clients involved in the activity we were photographing if they would like to be in a film. Anyone who preferred not to be photographed took a break and watched the proceedings. Both the families and the clients were pleased with the idea of a film. The only complaints we got were "too bad Johnny was not in the film."

We paid a photographer to do the shooting but all other services were donated. We decided the value of the film would be enhanced by a good "voice." Floyd Kalber, then a leading Chicago area television newscaster and now a national newscaster, consented to do the narration. He made a tape in his television studio, reading the script in the timing we suggested.

The filming covered a three week time span and took about thirty hours of shooting time and twelve rolls of film, each roll representing five minutes of projection time. We, therefore, had sixty minutes of film from which to produce an eight minute finished product. It was barely enough.

The film was developed at no charge, and then we began the tedious and critical job of editing. Using the equipment at a professional film editing house, we edited the film to roughly fit the time narrative.

We then had a working print or "Dirty Dup" made of the film; we asked a professional film editor to synchronize the narrative to the working print. We selected a simple guitar music accompaniment for background and had a tape loop made of the music. A sound studio donated their services to mix the music with the narration, providing a softly muted musical background which enhanced the narrative and filled the places in the film which used only visual expression to communicate.

We then took the tape of music and narration to a specialist who made and contributed an optical print of the sound. The edited original film was matched to the optical print of the sound track and film processors donated their services to produce a finished 16 mm film with sound.

The debut for our $400, 16 mm film was the opening night benefit performance of Barbra Streisand's "Funny Lady."

The home-movie quality of our film contrasted with the multi-million dollar Streisand film was extremely effective, and all feedback from the audience was positive. In fact, a significant number of people felt the content of our film, its openness and sensitivity, made it the best of "show." However, it was an audience of supporters for the needs of disabled people and they may have been less than totally objective.

The individuals who donated their services to make the film were pleased they could help, each with his own unique talent, and offered to be available when an update was needed.

Both donors and viewers benefited from the film.

Chapter 14

LINK #3: COMMUNICATING THROUGH MASS MEDIA

EFFECTIVE media communication will enhance public education.

Each medium — newspapers, radio, television, and periodicals — has its own special characteristics.

A professional staff person experienced in mass communication, public relations, or media production is ideal to direct a mass media program. However, a volunteer committee of professionals in public relations, radio, television, and newspaper fields, working with the community education staff, is a highly acceptable substitute.

As in all other things relating to the community, the establishment of a personal rapport with a variety of individuals is helpful.

The first step, therefore, is to learn about all the newspapers, radio stations, and television stations which serve the area and then identify the key people, as well as their deadlines. It is important to speak with one voice. If several persons of the same organization make contradictory statements, it diminishes the credibility of the organization. The program starts by educating the editors and writers (see Chapter 8).

A six-month media program might include the following elements:

Television — The most difficult medium on which to gain exposure.

August — Feature Bonaparte school director on Cromie Circle (TV late night talk show).

November — Feature two Knights of Columbus and a staff person regarding lead poisoning detection and prevention on educational TV.

January — Send slide clips obtained from National Association for Retarded Citizens to all TV stations to stimulate membership drive contributions.

March — Arrange for an interview of a businessman who employs handicapped person in conjunction with the businessmen's campaign.

April — Feature cerebral palsied board member and executive director on United Cerebral Palsy telethon with Irv Kupcinet.

Radio

July — Have benefit committee chairman named "Lady of the Day" on WAIT.

September — Feature two mothers of handicapped teenagers on radio interview show.

October — Vocational placement counselor interviewed regarding advantages of hiring handicapped people.

February — Interview on need for subcontract work by workshops for handicapped.

May — Public service announcements urging people to attend spring benefit.

Newspapers — The medium which is potentially the best source for maximum exposure on the activities of human service agencies.

David Halvorsen, managing editor of the San Francisco Examiner, advises:

> Develop a sense of timing of the news. If a certain type of story breaks in the newspapers, be prepared to offer various staff experts who can background the subject. If a reporter learns about the talent on your staff, he or she will call on them for some insight. It is a very effective working understanding.
>
> If a controversial issue is coming up, take the initiative. Rather than risk erroneous or incomplete information appearing in print, visit the editors of the various key newspapers in your area to discuss what you are trying to do. Keep it low key and remember you are explaining your side of the issue and that you fully understand the editor must fairly present the story whether it is good or bad for your interests.
>
> On routine matters, send a press release, insuring that all go out in the mail at the same time.

Know the publishing dates of the newspapers in your area so that your press releases arrive before editing deadline. This is particularly critical for weeklies and semi-weeklies.

The newspapers pay reporters to write stories. Do not become enamored with your own writing style in preparing press releases. Just present the basic information and do it as briefly as possible.

If a newspaper publishes factual errors about your organization or projects, do not hesitate to call the editor and tell him about it. Errors should be corrected. Be certain you distinguish between errors in fact and the newspaper's interpretation. Seldom will you convince an editor that his interpretation is wrong unless you have established a working rapport and confidence with him beforehand.

Announcing publicity events too far in advance can be just about as ineffective as announcing them too late. Even if an item appears in a paper three months in advance, most people will forget about it. Think in terms of twenty to twenty-five days with necessary follow-up stories. Have ideas for the reporter who calls you looking for a story angle. Do not pander the cheap publicity stunt or compromise the principles of the handicapped's right to privacy. Publicity stunts went out of style with lace girdles and rumble seats. A good publicity stunt comes by only once in awhile now, and it is masterminded by a pro, not a bunch of amateurs sitting around the office thinking up ideas.

New programs, professional staff, disabled people, board members, volunteers, special events, results of studies, meetings, and new laws affecting disabled people can all be the subject for press releases or feature stories.

News surrounding conflict always seems to get more space and time. Disagreement is unfortunately more exciting to the public than harmony. Therefore, special attention must be paid to handling the release of information during a crisis.

Twelve *B*s of Dealing with the Media[1]

Be the only person to contact in your organization.

[1]National Association of Retarded Citizens Conference Las Vegas, October 1975

Be quick to establish right department for your news item. This may change.

sports
society
news

Be sure of facts

Be prompt meeting deadlines

Be legible — type — double space everything. Do not use carbon copies for paper.

Be accurate — double check spelling and typing.

Be honest and impartial.

Be brief.

Be brave. Suggest new ideas.

Be businesslike — do not threaten.

Be appreciative — do not complain you only got two paragraphs.

Be professional — see if press badge needed, set up press conferences.

Chapter 15

LINK #4: SPECIAL TARGETS

SPECIFIC problems surrounding needs of handicapped people might require individual communication campaigns with special target groups.

The constituency can be drawn upon to furnish leadership for these campaigns and the media can be contacted for publicity and news coverage, but the primary method of communication should be person to person.

For example, the success of a new program designed to teach mothers how to stimulate the learning of their developmentally disabled child requires that the mother know her child is disabled and that she know of the availability of a program to help. A broad public information approach using the mass media will help but the primary consultant to a mother regarding her infant's health is the pediatrician or general practitioner to whom she relates. Therefore, general practitioners, pediatricians, public health nurses, and all other medical specialists relating to infant care became the target for communicating the beginning of our new program.

Question: "Who would doctors listen to?" Answer: "Another respected professional specialist with a similar educational level."

1. A personally typed letter from the director of children's services in our agency was sent to each doctor in the county who might be in contact with a family of a handicapped child.
2. A call was made to the county medical society requesting their suggestions for the most effective means of communicating with doctors personally. Their recommendation was to request permission from each hospital's medical director to have the director of children's services and the infant program director speak at a pediatric staff meeting. This advice was followed and the request granted. Referrals

to the program increased dramatically.
3. A similar presentation was made to all the public health nurses.
4. Follow-up mailings to doctors and public health nurses were done at six-month intervals to update information regarding the program and resupply them with pamphlets on the program.

There are two *whos* in the usual who, what, where, when, how, and why of communication in addressing special audiences. One is to whom are we communicating and the other is to whom will the audience listen. The choice of communicator will vary according to the audience. It may be a respected peer or an accredited peer in an allied field, a wealthy, powerful, or politically influential member of the community, a respected member of the lay community, or someone who has used the services.

The where, when, how, and why must be given equal consideration. The right place, the right time, the right method, and the right reason are all there, they only require discovery and implementation.

Attorneys and Trust Officers

Families of handicapped children were confused about how to provide for the well-being of their disabled child when the parents died. Many times the parents felt that the majority of their assets should be designated for the welfare of their handicapped offspring, rationalizing that the "normal" offspring were better equipped to meet their own needs. Yet, when talking to other parents, they found that all assets held in trust for the disabled child must be depleted before tax dollars were made available even in the state facilities. The effect of estate planning on the family was therefore negative. The well-being of the disabled child was not enhanced and the other members of the family were left with diminished resources.

Establishing a forum for the exchange of information among trust officers and attorneys became a priority. Since the two groups did not meet together with any regularity, a luncheon seminar was planned featuring an attorney-trust officer who was dealing successfully with the issue in another city.

A prominent attorney in the organization's constituency was selected to chair the meeting and notify other attorneys of the seminar through the local bar association's newsletter. Not having a trust officer actively involved in the constituency, the director of public education wrote to the trust officer at each bank in the county to invite them to the seminar.

A moderate fee covering the cost of the luncheon was charged.

Chapter 16

LINK #5: USING VOLUNTEERS AND ADVOCATES AS COMMUNICATORS

IN our highly mechanized, relatively affluent society, people search more ardently than ever for meaningful involvement. There is more opportunity than ever to develop challenges for them in volunteer work. The executive who daily directs research projects aimed at determining how many raisins to put in each cereal box, the assembly line production worker, the widget salesperson, and the housewife or houseperson frequently wonder if their "work" really has significance. Many share the need to feel they have done something of real value for someone else. The human service agencies operating in the community can help them meet that need.

To use a very old cliche, the most effective means of communication ever developed are telephone, telegraph, television, and tell-a-woman. The last should more appropriately be tell-a-person simply because children and adults, male and female, communicate constantly as part of their lives. Every person is potentially a volunteer advocate for the needs of handicapped people. A volunteer advocate is anyone who helps in any way advance the cause of expanding choices and opportunities for handicapped people. A strong corps of volunteers and advocates can carry the message that the large majority of handicapped people can lead meaningful, productive lives; that opportunities for employment need to be developed; that architectural barriers need to be removed; that public attitudes need to continue to change to create an atmosphere of understanding and acceptance; that legislative changes need to be effected; that local citizens need to support community agencies involved in providing both direct and indirect services to handicapped people; that handicapped people have a right to have their human and citizen rights protected; and that people who may or may not be handicapped can meet their own needs by helping others.

Direct service volunteers can obviously play a vital role in helping create opportunities for the development of handicapped people. However, a more subtle but equally vital role is available to all those who would like to help, but "just can't work in a classroom full of disabled children." If these interested people can be recruited, organized, and taught to conduct a continuing education program in the community, the movement of mentally handicapped people from institutions into the community will be more smoothly conducted, the integration of visibly and invisibly handicapped people into the mainstream of life will be easier.

The information communicated to the volunteers about handicapped people, their problems and capabilities, the services that are available, the services still needed, should be totally honest and relayed in relatively simple terms, rather than in "professionalese." In other words, the *philosophy* should be taught rather than the *technicalities*. The teaching setting can be social or educational.

Once the volunteers are acquainted with the philosophy and become *volunteer spokesmen,* they can nurture a passing interest in a businessman employing handicapped people into a reality by introducing the appropriate staff member to the businessman at the appropriate time. The volunteers become links throughout the community between the professional staff, the client, and the lay public. As the links increase in number, the public becomes more widely educated.

The crucial point in this communication system is obviously the staff person,

PROFESSIONAL STAFF ——→ COMMUNICATOR ——→ VOLUNTEERS

who is responsible for relaying information from the professional staff to the volunteers.

Just as the term "gigo" (garbage in-garbage out) is used in

computer programming, so too does it apply to programming information to the public. If volunteers are circuits of communication, they must receive accurate, real information.

SECTION IV

The Issues In Rehabilitation and Habilitation

Chapter 17

EXPLAINING THE ISSUES IN REHABILITATION AND HABILITATION

Rehabilitation and Habilitation

To rehabilitate means to restore. To habilitate means to enable. If an individual has lost the ability to function in a specific area, such as sight, hearing, use of arms or legs, speech, or intellect, it is possible to use rehabilitation programs and techniques to restore, compensate, or replace that ability. If the individual is physically disabled or mentally retarded from birth, he requires not rehabilitation but habilitation. That which was never there cannot be restored. It can, however, be developed initially — this is habilitation.

The enabling programs and techniques may be the same in initial habilitation or in rehabilitation.

The Cost

The justification for diverting resources from other areas for use in habilitation and rehabilitation can be expressed in human costs and benefits, as well as material costs and benefits.

If resources were infinite, the only concern would be to develop the technology which would (1) prevent disabilities and (2) enable each already disabled individual to function maximally with all the supports needed to live a full and meaningful life. However, resources are not limitless; choices must be made and priorities established.

Who Pays for Disability

Our society places high value on the ability to cope, to be productive, to be physically and intellectually able, and to be attractive. When one loses any of those valued qualities through an accident, insurance settlements may be very high, enabling the victim to take advantage of the best treatment available. When one loses one of those qualities in the armed services, the government readily makes lifelong treatment and support systems available. However, if one is unlucky enough to be born with or somehow develop a disability or be disabled in an accident where no financial resources are available, the resources must come from the public sector. While a judge might award an individual $1,000,000 for the loss of the use of the lower half of the body, taxpayers (the public) may balk at giving each person born with a similar loss of ability an equal settlement.

Policy for Children

To encourge the family of a disabled child to keep the child with the natural family will cost society a great deal less. The cost of state-operated programs for severely retarded and multiply handicapped children is $25,000 a year per child,[1] exclusive of special education costs and exclusive of capital costs in constructing these facilities. Therefore, programs and policies which provide supportive services to the family — rent subsidy, the cost of a homemaker once a week, respite care if the family needs a vacation, provision of special equipment, and reimbursement for extraordinary medical expenses can easily be justified on a material cost-benefit basis. The cost of all these supports would be far less than the $25,000 a year it costs the public to provide care in a state-operated facility. The child would benefit from remaining with his natural family, providing the family can be taught and is willing to provide a natural home. If, however, the family cannot be taught or is unwilling to have the child in the natural home, forcing this policy would have high human costs. The mother or father might break down emotionally, siblings might suffer and the disabled child would have a high likelihood of being abused

---

[1]Illinois Department of Mental Health, 1975-76 Budget. Springfield, Illinois, Office of the Comptroller, March 1975.

emotionally or physically.

In these cases, the child is obviously better off not in the natural home. Since most research indicates child development is enhanced in a normal family setting, the environment duplicated should be a normal family setting. Alternatives to institutional care should be developed which have the goals of being either more beneficial to the disabled child's development or as beneficial but more cost efficient to society. For example, a well-planned and monitored system of specially trained foster parents which enables the disabled child to live in a normal family setting in the community when the natural home is not available can be an effective solution.[2]

Policy and Cost

Within that famework of restraints imposed by finite financial resources, rehabilitation policies and goals can easily be established for mildly and moderately disabled people. Maximum benefit for the largest number of disabled individuals can be achieved with the most efficient use of resources by helping only the mildly and moderately disabled individual since this is the group with the most potential to live normally and productively. Thus, the benefits of investing monies to help disabled individuals achieve an effective level of functioning benefits society because the mildly disabled individuals have a high likelihood of becoming contributing human beings as a result of rehabilitation. They repay the investment themselves through productive activities, i.e. competitive employment or homemaking and child-care which yield income. They become taxpayers rather than tax burdens and simultaneously produce goods or services for the consumption of others.

Clearly, rehabilitation programs for the mildly and moderately disabled can be justified on the basis of material cost benefit alone. The President's Committee on Employment for the Handicapped has found for every $1.00 invested in

[2]D. Rosen, Superintendent of the Institution Without Walls, Michigan Department of Mental Health.

vocational training for a handicapped individual, that person earns $14.00. Other studies have indicated for each $1.00 invested, the disabled person earns $29.00. The human benefit to the disabled individuals is immeasurable. There is no real way to measure the value of being able to live a full life.

Policy and Cost for the Severely Disabled

Policies and programs for the severely disabled individuals may require a different orientation. Such persons may never be competitively employed and may never earn enough money in sheltered employment to cover even a fraction of the cost of developmental programs. Yet the more self-help skills they learn, the less others will have to do to care for them; therefore, the lower the disabled person's cost to society.

The severely disabled, totally dependent person will cost society not only the material costs of total care and the loss of his contributions as a functioning human being, but also the loss of productivity in other persons who must care for him.[3]

While habilitation or rehabilitation programs for the severely disabled could result in development to the point of annual earnings of $10,000 a year per person, with exactly the right job to fit exactly the abilities which are possible for that individual, it may also cost $15,000 a year for special housing, transportation, and attendant or medical care for that individual. More likely earnings for this population might be $600[4] a year and costs of living — housing, food, attendants, transportation, and recreation — could be $20,000 a year. Policy decisions should focus on funding programs which result in the greatest benefit to this population at the most efficient cost to society. Thus an institutionalization program may cost $20,000 a year and a system of services in the community might cost $10,000 a year per person. If the disabled person can develop more effectively in the community and if he chooses that alternative, it is clearly less expensive to society and more effective for the disabled

[3]R. W. Conley, *The Economics of Vocational Rehabilitation* (Baltimore, Maryland, The Johns Hopkins Press, 1965).

[4]Ray Graham Association Workshop Levels 3 and 4, Addison, Illinos. Ray Graham Association Annual Report, 1975-76.

individual to utilize community services. In some instances, the disabled person may have gotten used to an institutional setting and is afraid to face the challenges of life in the community. In these cases, life in an institutional setting better meets the needs of the disabled person even though it might have a higher material cost. Since the institutional syndrome is the result of previous solutions to a social problem, it is society which created this dependency; therefore, it is society which must bear the additional cost.

Future Planning

The future planning of services should take into consideration the research results which indicate that institutionalization intensifies handicaps and reinforces dependency. A large proportion of patients in mental hospitals are kept there for largely social reasons — many attributable to institutionalism (Ullman, 1967[5] Scheff, 1963,[6] Brown, 1959[7]).

K. W. Cross (1957)[8] found the supervisory character of the hospital was as much a product of tradition as it was a response to the needs of the patient.

A. B. Cooper and D. F. Early (1961)[9] concluded that a majority of the 1,000 long-term patients they surveyed did not require custodial care and that a majority could work. These researchers all felt the handicaps of the institutionalized disabled person were intensified — that their ineffectiveness was reinforced rather than their ability to develop. The institution may be a comfortable and safe environment freely chosen by some disabled individuals, but it is neither cost effective nor developmentally desirable for many disabled people.

---

[5]L. P. Ullman, *Institution and Outcome Comparative Study of Psychiatric Hospitals* (New York, Pergamon Press, Inc., 1967).

[6]T. Scheff, "Legitimate, Transitional and Illegitimate Mental Patients in a Midwestern State," *American Journal of Psychiatry,* September 1963.

[7]G. Brown. "Social Factors Influencing Length of Hosptial Stay of Schizophrenic Patients," *British Medical Journal, 2,* December 1959.

[8]K. W. Cross. "A Survey of Chronic Patients in a Mental Hospital," *British Journal of Psychiatry, 103,* January 1957.

[9]Q. B. Cooper and D. F. Early. "Evolution in the Mental Hospital: Review of a Hospital Population," *British Medical Journal, 1,* June 1961.

As David Mechanic[10] says in *Mental Health and Social Policy*, "To insulate persons from events that encourage the development of new skills and the opportunity to practice them, undermines their capacity to deal with adversity and in the long run may be conducive to social and psychological breakdown."

Community based services should be the direction for service delivery systems because they are more cost efficient and because there is no substitute for teaching how to cope with life in the mainstream anywhere but in the mainstream. Institutional programs should be maintained only for specialized treatment of those dangerous to themselves and society and for those who have become so dependent on it because of past treatment they cannot or will not function anywhere else.

Human Profit versus Material Profit

Organizations with a purpose of human profit (human growth, improvement of skills, human development) have an inherent conflict if they are also operated for material profit.

If an organization must return dollars to investors, the bottom line in its operation is how much profit is available to distribute to investors. Investors do not want to receive a piece of paper which says: Income $1,000,000; expenses $1,000,000; profit 100 people moved out, went off welfare, got jobs, became self-supporting. The private investor's purpose in putting up his material wealth was to generate income for himself, not society as a whole. It may make him happy that he helped someone else but not at the expense of perpetually losing dividends. When an organization operates a program for human profit and must choose between using its resources to improve the quality of the program or paying out dividends, the choice must be to repay investors. If the investors are private for-profit entrepreneurs that means pay dividends. If the investor is the public — or its representative a not-for-profit community agency — the repayment to investors is the human gain. If the

[10]D. Mechanic, *Mental Health and Social Policy*, (Englewood Cliffs, New Jersey, Prentice Hall, 1969).

beneficiary of human development is society as a whole, then the investor must also be society as a whole — not for-profit investors.

Ownership of capital facilities by private investors with a *reasonable* return on investment with the program operation by a nonprofit organization paying reasonable rent for use of the facility can be an appropriate compromise or partnership between for-profit and not-for-profit organizations. Most tax benefits accrue to the private owner, and those tax benefits may actually make it less costly for property ownership to be held by the for-profit private sector than by the public sector or the not-for-profit private sector. However, monitoring would be necessary to see that the return was *reasonable* and not excessive.

Recognition must also be given to the difference between programs with a goal of maintaining skills and those designed to develop skills. When human development and growth has reached its maximum feasible level, it is possible to care for or employ disabled people in an enterprise which has a profit motive, providing appropriate standards for licensing and programming are applied in the operation. In other words, the severely disabled people who cannot be placed in competitive employment could be employed in workshops doing specialized subcontract work with high profit margin and little learning value. Disabled or elderly people who have little chance of becoming independent and yet require a good deal of care in housing, might reside in a facility operated by a for-profit enterprise. Safeguards must be employed through monitoring and advocacy to see that human needs are met.

The Rights of Society

Rehabilitation policy decisions should reflect that society has the right to be protected from people who are dangerous and the right to choose how much of their own resources as individuals can be donated for rehabilitation.

Society also has the right, collectively through voting and citizen participation, to choose how much is paid out in taxes for rehabilitation or habilitation purposes. Society does not have the right to prevent the disabled person from functioning as a citizen in a free society.

The Rights of the Disabled Individual

Rehabilitation policy decisions must reflect equal consideration for the rights of the disabled individual. The right to choose is basic in a democratic society. Rehabilitation programs must provide alternatives. It is highly desirable to develop programs which encourage independence, but it may also be necessary to provide dependence if that is the psychological, emotional, or physical need of the individual established by past experiences and practices of society as a whole or by institutionalization.

It is the rights of the disabled individual which need protection, not the disabled individual. Traditions and practices which smother the disabled person in the name of protection are a violation of their rights as citizens. The disabled person must choose at what point on the dependence-independence scale he wishes to live. No rehabilitation program, no matter how technologically perfect or materially expensive, can succeed without the cooperation of the individual it was designed to benefit. The disabled person can be given opportunity but he must want to take advantage of that opportunity. Once the barriers are diminished, failure or success at living is truly the choice of the individual.

SECTION V

Fund Raising and Support Organizations

Chapter 18

FUND RAISING FOR HUMAN SERVICE AGENCIES

"Nothing but what you volunteer has the essence of life, the springs of pleasure in it. These are the things you do because you want to do them, the things your spirit has chosen for its satisfaction."

Woodrow Wilson
Princeton, June 13, 1909

INADEQUATE financial resources frequently inhibit the initiation or operation of needed programs. Raising money through voluntary contributions can help alleviate that program. However, there is a special challenge involved in raising money to help people who have problems that most people would prefer did not exist.

Fund raising, properly done, can and should be used both as a resource for money and as a tool to achieve the social action necessary to create an appropriate developmental climate in the community.

Too often agencies raising money for programs for disabled people use approaches which are in conflict with the goal of protecting human dignity and creating an atmosphere for acceptance and growth for disabled people.

The fund raising propaganda frequently perpetuates the concept of "helplessness" as being synonomous with disabled. Many professional fund raisers say, "You must evoke sympathy, then people give. Make 'em cry and the money rolls in." It is critical that fund raising be integrated with programmatic goals.

Since it is necessary to educate and involve people to really gain acceptance for the needs and rights of handicapped people and since one means of involving people is through fund raising activities, the appropriateness of a fund raising technique for handicapped people should meet certain criteria:

1. Does it preserve the dignity and rights of the disabled people it is designed to benefit?
2. Does it convey a positive image? "Invest in the development of human potential" rather than, "Won't you help those less fortunate than you?"
3. Is it educational rather than exploitative? Does it help create a real understanding of the needs and potential of disabled people?
4. Does it honestly state for whom and for what the money will be used?
5. Is there a plan of action — a goal, a timetable, appropriate leadership?
6. Does all the written material and spirit of the campaign or event coincide with the programmatic goals and philosophy of the agency?
7. Will recognition be given to the volunteers for their efforts during and after the campaign or event?
8. Have the contributors been thanked for their gifts?
9. Was the campaign or special event a positive experience for all who were involved?

All plans for involvement of people in the community should be designed to reward both the volunteer and the program for handicapped people. Exploitation of givers and volunteers is no more appropraite than exploitation of handicapped people.

If the involvement results in positive feelings, interest will be maintained and a larger and larger base of support can be built.

Harold J. (Si) Seymour is often called "the most quoted man in the field" of fund raising. He is one of the founders, a past president, and an honorary member of the American Association of Fund Raising Council.

In his book, *Designs for Fund Raising,* Mr. Seymour summarizes fund raising techniques as follows:

1. Effective fund raising is never easy, but it can always be simple: get the dedicated advocates committed by their own words, deeds, and gifts; organize to achieve reasonable coverage; then aim all your promotion, in an atmosphere of pride and responsible concern for continuity, toward the arts of good conversation.
2. All campaigns should create and sustain the mood of relevance, importance, and urgency, with an attitude of faith and confidence.
3. Program should always be kept ahead of fund raising in everything planned and all you do. Sell the opportunities and not the deficiencies, never forgetting that money flows to promising programs and not to needy institutions.
4. Every good campaign is essentially a public relations operation — an aggregate of the tremendous trifles by which any enterprise wins and holds public approval: good manners, pleasurable experiences, recognition for achievement, and proof that all the sacrifice anyone made was worth far more than it cost.
5. Never fear pressure. Seek it out and use it in full and cheerful measure. Without its leverage, in terms of quotas and deadlines, nothing will move and your campaign will languish and die.
6. Perhaps above all, give every step a plan and every move a timing. If all else goes blank, just remember that the essence of it all is that somebody, with some good reasons, has to see somebody about giving some money for the advancement of some good cause.

A community education program must precede fund raising because people will only give money after they know who you are and what you do. The act of generating support then becomes an extension of the education process and becomes part of the social action plan.

In the following chapters is an outline of a variety of fund raising techniques:

1. *Membership campaigns* (see Chapter 21): good for community education; medium good for involvement; medium cost effective.
2. *Special events* (see Chapters 19 and 20): excellent for

involvement; medium cost effective.

3. *Mass mailings* (to lists purchased from specialists): possibly good for education; poor for involvement; the least beneficial cost ratio (most expensive means of raising money).

4. *Selling Christmas cards:* possibly good for education and creating a positive beautiful image; poor in cost effectiveness for local organization; better cost effectiveness if measured in monies raised for both national chapter and local chapter.

5. *Community Chest or United Way participation* (see Chapter 17): use audio-visual presentations and tours; excellent for involvement; excellent in cost effectiveness and in-depth education to United Way volunteers and corporate executives; fair in effectiveness for broad community education; good for speaking engagements to employees of corporations.

6. *Local tax dollars* (see Chapter 19): good opportunity for in-depth education of elected officials; can be excellent means for broad community education initially when establishing need; after tax levy is imposed to meet need, awareness declines; a need met is no longer as newsworthly.

7. *Capital campaign for special gifts:* use small private gatherings, private tours, and one-to-one discussions; good for in-depth education and involvement of wealthy individuals; excellent in cost effectiveness; especially good for starting new programs or acquiring buildings and equipment.

8. *Clubs and organizations:* ask for speaking engagements; use audio-visual presentations and tours; good for providing exposure of services; broad education; good to excellent for involvement and support; good cost effectiveness; fit club's area of interest to handicapped people's needs.

9. *Grants from private foundations:* requires considerable research to match needs of agency programs with priorities currently being funded; best chances for funding are for new, innovative projects that match foundations current priorities; information on current priorities is best obtained from staff or directors of the private foundation.

Fund Raising and Accountability: Sample Cost Benefit Analysis

Community Chest

Costs

Preparation of application		
Client records 2 full-time staff members	1 month	$2,000.00
Bookkeeper — full-time	1 month	1,000.00
Recruitment, training, and supervision of volunteers		
Attending	120 hours @ $4	480.00
Presentations to Chests	40 hours @ $8	320.00
Acknowledgement monthly of allocations — clerical and supervisory	120 hours @ $4	480.00
Printing costs for applications		200.00
Executive contact with Chest personnel and boards	100 hours @ $8	800.00
Tours for Community Chest campaign workers		
Speeches at corporate campaign meetings 1 full-time	2 months	1,600.00
		$6,880.00

Revenue

Allocation 1974 — $ 70,000
1975 — $100,000

Cost 1975 6.8%
Return 1975 $14.70 for each $1 invested

Costs

Revenue Sharing — Local Tax Dollars

Research, data gathering, preparation, and presentations	300 hours @ $8	$2,400.00
	20 hours x 12 months = 240 hours x $4	960.00
	20 hours x 12 months x $3	720.00
		$4,080.00

Revenue

1974 Allocation $100,000	Cost 4.08%	Return $24.50 for each $1 spent
1975 Allocation $160,000	Cost 2.55%	Return $39.00 for each $1 spent

Return $39 for each $1.00 spent

Fund Raising Through Special Events

Costs

Art Show	1 full-time staff @ $700.00	2 months	$1,400.00
	Clerical part-time staff @ $500.00	2 months	1,000.00
	Proceeds to Artists		3,000.00
			$5,400.00

Revenue

1975 Income $8,000.00

Cost 67%

Return $1.47 for each $1.00 invested

Dinner Dances

Costs

1 full-time executive staff	529 people Dinner Dance # 1	518 people Dinner Dance # 2
6 weeks @ $175 a week	$ 1,050	$ 1,050
1 clerical part-time staff 6 weeks @ $150	900	900
Music and entertainment	960	1,300
Printing and postage	722	900
Catering	6,189	7,875
Other miscellaneous	1,649	
	$11,470	$12,025.00

Income

General Tickets @ $12.50		$ 1,750
Tickets @ $30		8,580
Tickets @ $50	$3,950	4,850
General Tickets @ $18.75	8,175	
Contributions	2,282	13,318
Bar	3,833	2,865
	$18,240.00	$31,363.00
Net Profit	$ 6,770.00	$19,338.00

Costs for Dinner Dance # 1 66% Return $1.51 for each $1 invested
Costs for Dinner Dance # 2 45% Return $2.19 for each $1 invested

Housewalk

Costs

Ticket printing, pictures, police	$1,753.38
Advertising programs, printing	596.36
Payments to artist for art sold	1,046.34
	$3,396.08

Revenue

Ticket sales	$ 9,688.50
Advertising program	3,280.00
Boutique and art sales	1,979.00
Bake sales	1,309.25
Contributions	374.03
	$16,630.78

Return $5 for each $1 invested

Capital Campaign

Costs

Capital campaign	160 hours @ $8 staff time	$1,280.00
Special gifts	80 hours @ $4	320.00
		$1,600.00

Revenue

Glos	$10,000
Hanson	10,000
Hall	10,000
Bates	7,500
Meyers	10,000
Dunteman	7,500
Proceeds	$55,000

Cost 3%

Clubs and Organizations Including Knights of Columbus

Costs

Expenses Staff time, speeches, helping recruit volunteers, publicity	200 hours @ $8	$1,600.00
	40 hours @ $4	160.00
		$1,760.00

Revenue

Cost 10%

Membership Campaign

Costs

1 full-time staff	
160 hours @ $8	$1,280.00
1 full-time secretary	
160 hours @ $4	480.00
Printing for mailing	200.00
Postage	200.00
Luncheon	288.00
Photos	172.50
TOTAL EXPENSES	$2,620.50

Revenue

Businessmen's luncheon	$5,925.00	
Patten Industries received July 1975 from businessmen's luncheon	1,000.00	
Total from businessmen's luncheon	$6,925.00	$6,925.00
Organization scholarship contribution proceeds		
Oak Brook Rotary Club		1,200.00
Elmhurst Kiwanis		600.00
Regular membership contributions		4,745.00
TOTAL PROCEEDS		$13,470.00

Cost 17%

Return $6.00 for each $1.00 invested

Foundation Grant

Costs

Research, phone conversations, tours, information gathering, preparation, and presentation	Executive staff time 160 hours @ $8	$1,280.00
	Secretarial time 80 hours @ $4	320.00
		$1,600.00

Proceeds $50,000

Cost 3 1/3 percent

Return $31.00 for each $1.00 invested

Factors Involved in Maximizing Support From Community Chests or United Funds — "To be in or not to be in — that is the question"

Community Chest or United Fund support constitutes a significant endorsement of the services provided by an agency in the community. Across the country, boards of directors of "Community Funds" are faced with the difficult task of assessing the value of the services provided to the community by a number of different levels of organizations.

The boards are struggling to give health, education, and welfare services priority in funding, while satisfying the demand for funds from the traditional recipients of the funds such as Boy Scouts, Girl Scouts, Campfire Girls, YMCAs, etc.

Since the numbers of people served by a mental health/mental retardation/developmental disability agency are miniscule in comparison to the numbers of people served by scouting, etc., it is imperative that the rehabilitation agency build a strong case for support from the United Fund based on logic rather than emotion.

In addition to filling out the required forms with accompanying budgetary data, there are some statistics necessary to build a strong case for the support of programs for handicapped people in your community:

1. Number of hours of service given to each community by the agency (clients x hours per day in program x days programming actually received).
2. Total cost per client per year based on average daily enrollment.
3. Total cost per client per year based on total enrollment.
4. Average cost to taxpayers for each institutionalized client per year.
5. Lifetime cost to taxpayers for each institutionalized client per year.
6. Savings provided by delivering the service in the community.

7. Savings to taxpayers provided by helping the handicapped person earn part or all of his income so that he in turn can pay taxes to repay the initial investment in him.

Some Community Chest members occasionally take the position, "Why help so few?" or "Why spend our money on handicapped people?"

It must be emphasized that choice between spending money on the handicapped or not does not exist.

If the local community does not provide support, the necessary services will have to be provided in an institutional setting at a much higher long-term cost to the taxpayers and possibly at the human cost of restricting the development of disabled people.

The appeal for support can be based on helping the handicapped person maintain his dignity by learning to be as independent as possible and on the fiscal wisdom of "investing" in providing services for the development of handicapped people in the community, in order that they may have the greatest opportunity to develop and, therefore, have the greatest opportunity to become contributing members of society.

Accurate statistics regarding clients are essential. You must be able to report

(1) how many clients from each community are in each program in a twelve month period and
(2) how many clients from each community have been moved into public schools, employment, or elsewhere.

Use examples adapted to your community and state such as: One handicapped person who is employed for $6,000 a year, will pay $40,000 in income tax in forty years; one handicapped person who is institutionalized for forty years costs the taxpayers $240,000 for a minimal level of care.

The choice is in the hands of the community. Shall we invest hundreds of thousands of dollars to isolate a handicapped person from society, or shall we invest a few thousand or perhaps even $20,000 to train him to become as independent as possible and perhaps permit him to earn $6,000 a year, thereby paying back double our investment in him in tax dollars while being a productive member of society.

We will do all we can by using our professional skill to train handicapped people, but we cannot do it effectively without your support.

Funds raised through the community chest approach have a very favorable cost benefit ratio compared with other voluntary contributions. If the restrictions placed on the agency by United Way seriously impede other fund-raising activities, the board must decide if United Way support is adequate to compensate for other lost opportunities. Our own experience has been positive because the Chicago Crusade of Mercy has taken the position that they cannot meet all the voluntary dollar needs of social and welfare agencies. They, therefore, encourage their participating agencies to raise money through special events, membership campaigns, and from individuals. The restrictions imposed require no fund-raising activities at any time during the Crusade of Mercy campaign, approximately sixty days a year, and no solicitation of corporations. On occasion a capital fund campaign is permitted for community-wide fund raising. The Chicago Crusade of United Way has found that individual agencies raising some of their own funds, raise their own visibility and therefore validate the way the Crusade is distributing its funds. This reciprocal arrangement is felt to increase the money pledged to the Crusade just as the individual agency's statement that it receives funds from the United Way helps legitimate the agency's status.

The Metropolitan United Way and Provider Agencies[1]

Metropolitan and other United Ways (and for-profit corporations) that are becoming potential leverage centers for community renewal have certain characteristics. They can successfully move people to action; they are adaptable and can change their names, symbols, and structures easily; they have low overhead; they are member-participant-client oriented

[1]Reprinted from S. Cousins, Executive Director of the New United Way Organizational Structure, monograph for The Metropolitan United Way and Provider Agencies, December 1976.

rather than organizationally occupied; they are mobile and can take risks in the economic, social, political, and spiritual arena. Their executives are planners, interpreters, community organizers, and are capable of broad inter-agency involvement and commitment. Their independent, voluntary organizational framework provides the base for formulating community goals that can help transform our cities into livable, workable, productive, democratic entities. Their objectives exemplify the aggregate spirit of the programs offered through their provider units. Their central management assumes the competence of branch operators. Their support systems are geared to the expressed needs of neighborhoods and are devised to free staff people in these neighborhoods to create new programs with and for the participants. A decisive characteristic of community transforming organizations is the healthy renewing of programs primarily at the neighborhood level — programs that are extensions of their objectives.

Reality Relationships — The United Way and Provider Agencies

ASSUMPTIONS:

1. The United Way will continue to be the major steward of the local community accountability system in private social welfare.
2. The United Way will continue to serve as a stimulator of human service program activity.
3. Local United Ways and their member agencies will have a jointly devised accounting and reporting system.
4. Increasingly, community-contributed dollars administered by the United Way will go for program services to alienated groups whether they be in the inner city or suburbs.
5. The improvement of relationships between the United Way and providing agencies and collaboration between the organizations can only be effectively developed on a local basis — town by town, city by city.

UNITED WAY CHALLENGES: In the years ahead, there are some specific challenges facing the United Way through its local operations

1. The need for increased United Way dollars for growing program services (8 percent to 10 percent a year minimum).
2. The rising expectations of
   a. Donors — for program accountability and low fund-raising costs.
   b. Effective agencies — for more reward dollars.
   c. Minority groups — for a greater share of the total dollars.
   d. All participants — for quality services.
3. A unified private social welfare system
   a. Planning, fund-raising, allocation priorities.
   b. Collaboration with public and private organizations.

CURRENT UNITED WAY PRIORITIES: In addition to an ongoing priority to increase fund-raising potentials in every United Way community, the United Way of America, through its "house of accountability" concept, is urging upon its local affiliates the utilization of stronger accountability systems. (This priority is in response to the rising expectations noted above in item 2.) Three of the "house of accountability" tools are of particular interest to most United Way local organizations:

1. UWASIS (or a comparable program service classification system)
2. *A Basic Accounting Guide*
3. A priority system for allocations

United Way locals across the country are subscribing in growing numbers (starting with the large city units) to the accounting guide and its basic chart of accounts. A priority system for allocations built on a program service classification system will be the most important thrust in the accountability area in the immediate years ahead. (Special note: most agencies, with their diversity of program and ability to adapt to changing community needs, should react favorably to a priority system of allocations and, at the same time, have impact on the content of the priority system itself.) As community-determined priority systems emerge as United Way policy — the list of controversial issues compelling the interests of the United Way and provider agencies will diminish in significance (i.e. supplemental fund-raising, reserve policies, depreciation, reporting demands, etc.). Agencies will decide whether or not to offer programs supporting the United Way priority system — depending on local objectives. At the same time, United Ways will be more interested in the purchase of specific priority program services and less interested in other areas of agency administration and program activity.

TRANSCENDENT ISSUES: United Way of America leadership, in concern with major national agencies, will be developing a more unified response to external pressures affecting both the United Way local organizations and their member agencies. Government program substitution, tax reform, and community expectations for quality services at a reasonable cost will occupy the energies of both our organizations and will far outweigh our preoccupation with intra-family issues. The basic effectiveness of voluntarism is at stake — and all participants in private social welfare must act in concern to insure the continuation of the private option in solving social problems.

ATTITUDES: Fundamental to a common strategy for survival and effectiveness is an examination of our mutual attitudes. A typical provider agency position of "The United Way is only a small part of our income and we can do without the Fund and its demands at any time," coupled with a typical United Way attitude "We live by the Golden Rule — those who have the gold make the rules," are counter-productive behaviors. Moving from these shortsighted attitudes to positions of collaboration and a unified private social welfare force will insure our common effectiveness in the years ahead.

Suggested Other Readings

American Association of Fund Raising Council, Inc.: *Giving U.S.A.* annual handbook, New York.

Arthur Anderson & Co.: *Tax Economics of Charitable Giving*. Subject File Co., 0500, item 31.

Bremner, Robert H.: *American Philanthropy*. Chicago, University of Chicago Press, 1960.

Fund Raising Management. Garden City, New York. $8.00 per year, magazine 6 times per year.

Marts, Armand C.: *The Generosity of Americans*. Englewood Cliffs, New Jersey, Prentice-Hall, Inc., 1966.

Mirkin, Howard R.: *The Complete Fund Raising Guide*. Public Service Materials Center, New York.

Sheridan, Phillip G.: *Fund Raising for the Small Organizations*. Philadelphia, Evans, M. & Co., Inc., 1968.

Chapter 19

GETTING A SHARE OF LOCAL TAX DOLLARS

DETERMINE how much money has been allocated to each local governmental unit, city, county, and township or region for the type of services you offer.

Call each local governmental unit for information regarding procedure for making application. If no answer, go to a public meeting and ask for information regarding application for funds.

Meet individually and in small groups with local politicians involved in disbursing funds to explain the need and gain their support. Devote special attention to educating and involving the elected officials. Find out if your local unit has tax levying ability for the services needed. Funds can only be used for those areas of concern which the local governmental unit has the power to fund through state and local statutes.

Services to the disabled is a national priority for the use of revenue sharing, but local governmental units may not be able to fund those areas because of statutory limitations. If this is so, initiate state and local legislation to expand their ability.

Finally, local governmental units are directed by local politicians. All politicians respond to voters. Therefore, secure as much grass roots support as possible from local residents. Set up a timetable for the most effective display of support from voters. Most governmental units have hearings in addition to their regular meetings regarding the disbursal of revenue sharing funds. Have one articulate staff member put the request in at a formal hearing. If there is an annual town meeting, be sure the request is made again to the local governing board by other local residents.

Then follow up with appropriate local officials to initiate the grant process or an appropriate contract for services.

Chapter 20

THE VALUE OF SPECIAL EVENTS

Play[1]

We do not know when man begins to play. Play may start before birth, with the kicks and turns of the fetus; it certainly is present in the infant; and it continues throughout our lives.

When play is suppressed, both the individual and society suffer. When play is encouraged, both benefit. The reasons for this are not clear, but somehow play is essential for man and many other social animals.

Unlike most behavior, play has not been exhaustively studied. Scientists have difficulty taking it seriously. They argue about what play is. Some have narrow definitions; others would agree with Tom Sawyer that "Work consists of whatever a body is obliged to do. . . . .Play consists of whatever a body is not obliged to do."

Play has a major role in the natural history of many species. Some of the importances and intricacies of play may be summed up in a paraphrase of a popular saying:

"Play is healthy for children. . . .and other living things."

Why Create the Opportunity for a Festival

Work is a central value in the culture of the United States. Total adoption of Calvin's definition of work as a virtue in itself has created a culture typified by material wealth for a large segment of the population.

Economic recession creates massive psychic depression for the total adult population and rubs off on the children. A recession in church attendance creates a depression in the clergy but not the parish members. A decline in play and festivity is affirmed as being morally right because frivolity is out of place during such a dire time. Energy and resources must be con-

---

[1] *A Natural History Magazine Supplement Special,* December 1971.

served for more basic functions — work and productive activity.

Our cultural perception of needs and wants center around the material. Play is not productive. It does not produce something which can be sold or used by someone else.

A number of philosophers and sociologists are now pointing out that the displacement of man's need for recreation is creating a desert in our environment. To play, to fantasize, to rejoice in the celebration of life is an essential part of life. Those activities which enable us to step aside from everyday responsibilities and permit renewal of the spirit should be encouraged and supported rather than discouraged as wasteful.

It would seem true conservation of human resources would include creating an environment which provided the ingredients, in addition to the space and time, for maximizing human growth. Continued repetition of responding to demands centered around productive, rational behavior creates rigidity. Opportunities for fantasizing, changing roles, playing, reaching outside oneself in nonprescribed ways offers the means toward continued growth, increased flexibility, and creative experience. The vitality gained by individuals from such experiences will in turn revitalize our culture. While the product of play and recreation is not consumable by others, play is the means by which we feed the individual spirit which gives mankind the renewed zest to improve the quality of life in other areas.

Celebration as an affirmation of the goodness of life is both a positive and renewing force.

The dilemma, of course, is how does a society convey to its members who have placed such high value on work that not only is play okay, it should be encouraged?

How do we reintroduce the opportunity for festival — the celebration of life — when our religious mythology celebrates "feast days" on only a few occasions?

Josef Pieper[2] maintains that a true festival is rooted in religious beliefs — that the celebration of life transcends life here and now.

---

[2]J. Pieper, *In Tune with the World* (New York, Harcourt Brace & Janovich, Inc., 1973).

Harvey Cox[3] tells us that when culture was dominated by religion, we had a great deal of festivity and fantasy.

Huizinga[4] says play is voluntary. It is not real or ordinary — it is an extraordinary activity. It is an interlude. It is secluded and limited in time and space. It creates its own order. It is joyful activity. "Play precedes culture and is the basis for culture."

John Koval[5] says, "Our culture has come to use, as the indicator of civilized or uncivilized behavior for other cultures, the question, 'Do the adults play a lot?' The conclusion is, if they play a lot they are not civilized. 'They do not take life seriously.' If the measure of civilization is how many goods are produced, that question may provide rational criteria for such a judgment. However, if the measure of civilization is how good is the quality of life, how joyful are the people in that culture, the criteria for judgment is faulty."

If we can accept that life should have joyful experiences, and if we can accept that the celebration of life in festivals is an affirmation of the meaning and worthwhileness of life, then how can we legitimate the right and need to play now that religious feast days are so sparsely scattered in our culture.

The development of secular or quasi festivals might offer expanded opportunities for enriching life experience. The purpose of the quasi festival is to celebrate the joy of living.

According to Cox and Pieper, a true festival should have no utilitarian purpose. However, it would seem one way to move people back to the recognition that a festival is valuable would be by introducing a rational reason to have the festival. The initial legitimation for such a festival might well be to improve the quality of life for others.

For example, many negative attitudes toward mentally retarded, cerebral palsied, epileptic, and autistic people still need to be changed. In addition, programs must be developed in the community which are designed to enable disabled people

---

[3]H. Cox, *The Feast of Fools* (New York, Harper & Row, 1969).

[4]J. Huizinga, *Homo Ludens: A Study of the Play Elements in Culture,* Translated by R.F.C. Hull (Boston, Massachusetts, Routledge & Kegan Paul, Ltd., 1949), Chapter 12.

[5]J. Koval, Chairman, Dept. of Sociology, DePaul University.

to live in the mainstream of life.

What better way to connect positive beautiful feelings with helping disabled people than by sponsoring a quasi festival with the intent of raising funds to buy a group home, a small apartment building, etc., which will permit handicapped people to live in the mainstream of the community and develop to their maximum level of independence.

While the monies generated will certainly improve the quality of life for disabled people, attendance at the festival by the supporters and participants will be a joyful sensual experience, accompanied by the knowledge that their financial sacrifice (the price of admission) is helping their fellow man and can in turn improve the quality of each participant's life.

According to Koval[6] the characteristics of a festival include the following:

1. It is a joyful celebration.
2. It is a special time set aside from work and responsibility.
3. It is a time for play and fantasy.
4. There is overabundance, waste, and feasting.
5. The festival is a social and communal expression of shared values and a time of pleasure.
6. The pure festival is an activity engaged in for itself.
7. The quasi festival has a utilitarian purpose.
8. The festival may enlarge experience by reliving events of the past in the present.
9. Fantasy is a major ingredient in that fantasy is akin to hope — it prepares one for change. (It can prepare the way for the radical social change necessary for the deinstitutionalization of handicapped people.)
10. It is egalitarian and everyone at all social and economic levels participates.
11. Stimulants are used to release tension. Societal norms are dispensed with.
12. Costuming and staging encourage frivolous behavior.

To create a benefit/festival it would be appropriate to select a

[6]J. Koval.

theme which represents either another time or another place. Decorating the setting for the festival can be a source of great pleasure for the planners. The fanciful setting enhances the opportunity for those who attend the festival to step outside their everyday selves. Encouraging the participants to come in costume suggested to them by the theme, enhances the setting and further intensifies the willingness to play.

Interestingly, in our culture, when many fund raising benefits are held, ladies wear gowns which are costumes because they are not worn everyday but men must continue to wear suit, shirt, and tie — albeit sometimes the suit is a tuxedo.

If the benefit/festival permits women to dress fancifully, it should offer the same opportunity for men. For example, a Tahitian Tamarra (feast) permits women to wear sarongs, mumus, colorful gowns and men to wear everything from a loincloth to a pair of slacks and a shirt. Abundant green plants and flowers, shell necklaces for everyone as they arrive, tables covered with flowered fabric, candles, torches, native singers and dancers enhance the feeling of the extraordinary.

At an Oktoberfest everyone can be given their own souvenir stein at the door to fill with beer, soft drinks, or wine. Thueringer and sauerkraut, German dancers, musicians in liederhosen, participants dressed in their interpretation of German costume, arm wrestling contests for men and women, games of skill, more singing and dancing for everyone creates festivity.

A Zambra or gypsy feast might start by having pretty gypsies put a golden zlaga or earring on every man as he comes in to start the mood. Gypsy violinists, wild dancers, gypsy dishes from all over Europe, wine, riotously different colored cloths on all the tables, fortune tellers — mostly amateur — creates the opportunity for all to participate.

A barn raiser or country western party with an entrance through a mock corral, passing a mock graveyard of dead heroes and bad guys with wry prose on the headstones, square dancing, country music, sheriffs' badges for everyone, and jugs of cider on the table, again depart from our usual social events.

The point is to create an event which carries the feeling of something extraordinary and permits participation and celebration by everyone.

The advent of television has turned great numbers of citizens into observers rather than participants.

Participation has been sacrificed to the passive willingness to be entertained. Entertainment is more appropriately one component of play, not the totality.

People feel the need to express themselves in many different ways. The opportunities for that expression are extremely limited in our culture since all behavior, to be considered adult, is expected to be rational and rather sober. The creative, playful part of human behavior cannot be suppressed without sacrificing a loss in humanity, spirit, and vitality.

Doctors recognize the relationship between good health and a lifestyle which balances work and recreation. The concept of recreation as necessary for re-creation for all its validity is still perceived as frivolous. Perhaps when frivolity, play, recreation, and festivity are given a value in our culture on an equal basis with productivity, then the richness of life will again manifest itself.

Community agencies involved in providing human services can play a positive role in preserving the health of the total community by offering events with the material purpose of raising money to improve the quality of the service and with the spiritual purpose of enhancing the opportunities to celebrate the joy of living. The play activities can include the more traditionally interpreted festival held outdoors in the evening with food and drink, singing and dancing — such as the Tamarra, Zambra, or Barn Raiser — or it might be centered around entertainment — the opening night of a movie followed by a champagne, beer, or coffee party in the theatre lobby. It might be a pre-football-game foodfest, an international fair offering foods and entertainment from many countries, or a bowling party — whatever would best meet the needs and demands of the local community.

To be an advocate of play and festivity is to be a believer that life has meaning and is cause for rejoicing. Those who can celebrate most deeply are those who have endured pain. It is especially appropriate for groups of people concerned with improving the opportunity for handicapped people to live fuller, more meaningful lives, to advocate the means by which both able and disabled people in our culture may jointly celebrate the joy of living.

Chapter 21

HOW TO ORGANIZE A SPECIAL EVENT

SUCCESSFULLY operated special events can play a major role in developing support for both handicapped people and the agencies that serve handicapped people:

1. By gradually introducing the lay public to the very real needs, problems, and potentials of handicapped persons.
2. By making that introduction a positive experience.
3. By giving people a way to help in which they feel comfortable in their relationship to handicapped people and experience the reward of success.
4. By creating a different area of "news" to be carried by the media.
5. By associating "success" and "positive" and "helping" with handicapped people.

There have been volumes written about successful special events, but no one likes to talk about the unsuccessful events, so let us start with a list of *do*s and *don't*s.

*DO*s	*DON'T*s
Do preserve the dignity of handicapped people in requests for contributions and publicity.	Do not use a "pity the poor souls" or "Let's help the poor souls" approach.
Do promote the concept of providing the opportunity for each individual to develop to his maximum capacity.	Don't use the "the most we can hope to do for this group is. . ." approach.
Carefully select an event which is appropriate to the	Don't have a dinner dance for a group interested in bowling

cause and the community.	banquets.
Do have a boutique featuring revitalized or recycled cast-offs.	Don't have a rummage sale focusing on castoffs and second-rate goods.
Do have an arts and crafts sale, indicating the creativity of both handicapped and non-handicapped workers.	Don't exploit handicapped people and their products.
Do feature arts and crafts which sell on their own merit.	Don't offer second-rate hand-made items which sell because they were made by the handicapped.
Do give the special event the best you have in creativity and good management.	Don't have a limping benefit.
Do carefully project expenses and then add 15 percent for contingencies.	Don't spend more than 40 percent of projected income on producing the benefit.
Do establish quotas for tickets, advertising, patrons, items for sale, etc.	Don't tell ticket sellers, "sell whatever you can." Give them a goal.
Do decide how many volunteers you need, then recruit 20 percent more.	Don't invite people onto the committees just to lend their names.
Do assign reasonable responsibilities to each volunteer. Do, however, offer enough responsibility to challenge each volunteer.	Don't overburden the individual volunteer.

Do offer staff support and supervision. Insist on staff approval of all press releases, invitations, posters, letters of solicitation, and thank you letters.	Don't take the easy way out and let the volunteers run "wild."
Do maximize opportunities for publicity. Be aware of the deadlines of local newspapers in order to be of optimum service to the newspapers.	Don't forget to invite the press to announcement meetings.
Do maximize the opportunity to talk about the agency, its programs and its needs at a press party, an announcement party, and committee meetings.	Don't talk about the agency and its programs at the special event. People have come to have a good time and will resent a lengthy "commercial."
Do hire a photographer and prearrange whom you are going to photograph for at least two press party sessions. One session should be held two months before the event and one session held one month before the event.	Don't rely on the press to take their own photos. Although good papers want to take their own photos, good press coverage is assured if photographs are supplied by you.
Do have photos developed and mailed with a press release to *all* local publications.	
Do have a printed program for the event with information about the event, names of all	Don't forget to acknowledge all the donors of service (volunteer), money, and goods

committee members, donors, and advertisers. Insert literature on the agency or incorporate agency program information into the printed program.	in a printed program.
Do say "thank you" regularly to the volunteers and donors.	Don't forget to apply behavior and modification principles with the volunteers and donors by promptly rewarding positive behavior.

Volunteer Committees Needed

Honorary Chairman — Well-known, well-respected, possibly wealthy individual, who would prefer not to work on the nitty-gritty, but will bring a few large donations and prestige to the cause, and will be the catalyst for others to join the benefit committee. This is a very real help.

Benefit Chairman — Well-organized, natural leader, able to orchestrate the volunteers, smile at the donors, and work with the staff toward mutually established goals.

Patrons and Angels Chairman — Well-respected, preferably well-to-do person capable of motivating business people and other wealthy individuals or foundation principals to make large contributions to the cause. Special seating and recognition in the printed program are the rewards offered by the charity to Patrons and Angels. The reward to Patrons, Angels Committee members, is the prestige of being connected with the well-respected Patrons and Angels Chairman and his peers in assisting on a worthwhile project.

Reservations Chairman — On any event requiring reserved seating, ticket distribution should be handled by a Reservations Chairman. Preferably someone with a recognizable name, but most important with an orderly mind and a flexible nature.

The orderly mind is imperative for appropriate record keeping. The flexible nature is essential for the myriad last minute changes requested and for the "We would like to be seated next to ________ requests.

Advertising Chairman — An aggressive individual capable of motivating other volunteers to sell ads and equally proficient at persuading people to buy ads, always a good money maker assuming reasonable printing costs. (Have volunteers with advertising layout experience do the mock-up which a printer can photograph and print.)

Decorations Chairman — A creative but realistic person who substitutes creativity for large sums of money in creating the decor.

Ticket Chairmen — When a great many tickets (2,000-10,000) are to be sold to an event which does not require reserved seating, it is best to establish teams of ticket sellers for each community. This category of event would include a housewalk, and antique show, a craft show, an art show, etc. Because the "show" requires a large attendance, reasonably priced tickets ($2-$10 each) are best sold by distributing the tickets, numbered and accounted for, to team captains or ticket chairmen, who in turn distribute them to ticket sellers. The team captains are then responsible for accounting for both the unsold tickets and the money to the general ticket chairmen.

Benefit Committee — When tickets are sold through a reservations chairman, the accompanying volunteer structure would be recruited as a benefit committee. The responsibility of each benefit committee member is to "get a table of ten together" or encourage ten people to come. The benefit committee members mail invitations to their friends. The charity office mails invitations to its regular constituency, eliminating duplicates whenever possible.

Publicity

Since the special event has two main purposes — (1) to increase the visibility of the cause, (2) to generate money — it is preferable to have the staff handle all press releases and written or printed materials.

By all means, maximize the news surrounding the special event, but also maximize the media exposure for the cause itself — its name, purpose, goals, number of people served, locations, need for voluntary support, etc.

Staff Responsibilities

Assign a specific staff person, who relates well to volunteers, to guide and direct volunteer activities. Specify that all contractual arrangements must be in writing and signed by the appropriate staff person or the executive director. Specify that all written, printed, and published material must be approved by the staff before release. Make certain that existing insurance coverage is adequate; if not, arrange for special coverage (such as dram shop insurance for liquor sales) well in advance.

Establish a Timetable

SIX TO TWELVE MONTHS PRIOR: Appoint chairman.

SIX MONTHS PRIOR: Determine event.

FOUR MONTHS PRIOR: Select Executive Benefit Committee — begin contractual arrangements.

THREE MONTHS PRIOR: Announce benefit chairman and Executive Committee, recruit Benefit Committee members, arrange for printing.

TWO MONTHS PRIOR: Have a combination Benefit Committee meeting/press party for all Benefit Committee members and the press. Hire a photographer for this event. Give out tickets or invitations as well as a written description of event.

This should be a session to stimulate excitement and interest in your event. Use creativity in planning it. Hold the meeting at an interesting place. Use it as a prevue for the special event.

The primary purpose of the party/committee meeting is to make it a social event at which you communicate with *all* committee members and the media in person. The dynamics resulting from gathering everyone together will generate support and interest in your event and will multiply future support.

Two Months Prior: Have press releases for media, with names of committee members listed by community; announce goal — how many tickets, how many dollars net to be made.

Have chairman of Patrons and Angels Committee give a small luncheon for his committee members. Ask him to announce the size of his contribution, and one or two more, to motivate committee members in their efforts.

Following the press party, have photos developed and mail to appropriate media with press release. Oganize individual committee meetings to crystalize responsibilities and ideas.

One Month Prior: Be sure all contracts are finalized. Have final Benefit Committee meeting/press party. Announce more details, number of tickets sold (probably few), need to get down to business, names of special donors so far. Take more photographs at this event. Mail to the papers again.

Three Weeks Prior: Check with all committee chairmen on progress. If you have an advertising program, it should go to press now.

Two Weeks Prior: Count money. Meet with committee chairmen. Have telephone campaign to stimulate ticket sales.

One Week Prior: Keep in touch with committee chairmen. Step in or arrange for help for committees which may not be functioning.

If you have Angels and Patrons Committee, send copy for printed program to printer. Late additions can be included with a last minute supplemental sheet.

Three Days Prior: If this is a food event, give final count to caterer. Never guarantee more than you have collected money for. Caterers usually are equipped to serve 10 percent more, but if you guarantee the larger number, you will have to pay, even if people do not show up.

Special Event Day: Be there with extra help for last minute contingencies during set-up time. Have fun, smile at all the new faces.

Attached are several budgets for special events and final income and expense figures, as well as sample advertising forms.

Just as every person is unique, every committee is a unique combination of talent and personalities. The committee should work more effectively when the chairman is able to choose at least some of his own members. The group itself should have the freedom to accomplish their goal in their own way. People are always more committed to carrying out their own ideas and derive the maximum self-fulfillment when they are given the opportunity to do so.

In order to enable people to meet their own needs by helping others and simultaneously carry out organizational goals, a number of policies should be established by the organization which outline a framework within which volunteers can function satisfactorily.

For example, after running special events with staff leadership and volunteer participation for several years, the volunteers in our agency were anxious to assume a leadership role. However, the first special event they ran had very high costs attached to them. Since the volunteers considered the event more important than the fact that 60 percent of the proceeds were used up in costs, there was a conflict with the organizational goal of always keeping fund-raising costs at a minimum. In fact, several funding sources would withdraw funding if our own independent fund raising was economically inefficient.

A policy was therefore established by the board of directors which stated that all fund-raising activities conducted in the name of the association must have prior approval by the board. This included submission of the projected budget which must be followed. A staff member was then assigned by the executive director to work on the project with the volunteers. The role of the staff member was to see that the event was run in a manner not in conflict with the organizational goals established by the board. If a conflict arose the authority of the board of directors would be brought in to resolve it.

This organizational structure permits a staff member to work with board members on a committee even though the board members are technically his boss's boss. The policy, since it is adopted by the board to implement the achievement of organizational goals, acts as a monitor on everyone in the organization including the board members themselves.

Dear Friend,

Please accept our warmest thanks for donating for an advertisement in our "Program" to be distributed at our Spring Benefit.

Your contribution will enable us to continue providing developmental programs to help handicapped people lead fuller, more meaningful, and more productive lives in the mainstream of our communities.

Thank you.

Sincerely,

Sample Advertising Program Form

NAME OF ADVERTISER: ______________________________

ADDRESS: ______________________________

TOWN: ______________________________ ZIP: ____________

ADVERTISER'S SIGNATURE: ______________________________

VOLUNTEER SOLICITOR: ______________________________

PRICE SCHEDULE

CIRCLE ONE:

$10.00	. . . .	Listing . . . . one line
25.00	. . . .	1/8 page
50.00	. . . .	1/4 page
100.00	. . . .	1/2 page
200.00	. . . .	Full page
250.00	. . . .	Inside back cover

Copy as it will appear in program:

____

____

____

ALL CHECKS MADE PAYABLE TO: ______________________________

1 copy of contract to advertiser.
2 copies of contract to advertising chairman.

NAME OF ADVERTISING CHAIRMAN: ______________________________

ADDRESS: ______________ TOWN: ______________ ZIP: __________

TELEPHONE: ____________

Historical Housewalk
May 18 and 19, 1973

RECEIPTS:					
Tickets		$ 9,688.50			
Ads — program book		3,280.00			
Boutique		1,979.00			
Country store		1,309.25			
Contributions:					
Elmhurst Rotary	$268.53				
Harquardt security guard	65.00				
Other	40.50				
		374.03			
Total receipts to date				$16,630.78	
EXPENSES:					
Tickets:					
Pictures, artist, printers		$ 74.45			
Policeman		255.00			
Unique travel		268.53			
Postage		80.00			
C & L Photos		36.00			
Flowers — thank you		14.00			
Coffee and cake		896.59			
Change		75.00			
Petty cash		35.41			
Rental — cups		18.40			
Ticket expense			$1,753.38		
Program:					
Return ad		$ 50.00			
Printer		421.20			
Paper		125.16			
Program expenses			$596.36		
Boutique:					
Note paper		$ 162.71			
Artists		1,046.35			
Boutique expenses			$1,209.06		
Total expenses				$3,558.80	
Net proceeds					$13,071.98

"Mame"
March 28, 1974
Oak Brook Theatre Oak Brook, Ill.
As of 4/5/74

INCOME:			
Tickets:			
73 @ $50.00	$3,650.00		
725 @ $10.00	7,250.00	$10,900.00	
Advertising		3,120.00	
Champagne		162.00	
Donations		552.00	
	TOTAL INCOME		$14,734.00
EXPENSES:			
Seats		$2,740.00	
Photography		98.75	
Printing and paper		675.20	
Flowers		63.90	
Champagne		562.00	
Miscellaneous		45.00	
	TOTAL EXPENSES		$4,184.85
	Net profit		$10,549.15
Plus			
Uncollected income			
Ads	$1,000.00		
Tickets	40.00		
Flowers	52.00		$1,092.00
		TOTAL PROFIT	$11,641.15

Sample Income and Expense Sheet

EXPENSES

ANTIQUES		ART		BLACK TIE DINNER	
Printing	$730.20	Printing	$129.00	Printing	$49.2
Postage	23.69	Peg boards	32.00	Table wine	65.4
Travel reimbursement	33.40	Delivery of equipment	40.00	Florida trip	168.0
Newspaper ads	58.52	Miscellaneous	9.75	Pictures	61.0
Miscellaneous	12.00	Artist 80%	4,301.78	Orchestra	185.0
Sports Core 50%	3,370.00	Damaged painting	35.80	Sports Core	1,340.0
				Miscellaneous	9.7
SUBTOTAL	$4,227.81	SUBTOTAL	$4,548.33	SUBTOTAL	$1,878.4
Outstanding:		Outstanding:			
Sports Core	$66.00	Artist	$6.00		
Ushers	49.00	Sports Core	325.58		
Miscellaneous	5.25	Ushers	49.00		
TOTAL	$4,348.06	TOTAL	$4,928.91	TOTAL	$1,878.

INCOME

Tickets	$6,873.00	Sales	$4,007.50	Sales	$2,762.
Display ads	1,495.00				
Program books	254.80				
Bake sale	455.64				
SUBTOTAL	$9,078.44	SUBTOTAL	$4,007.50	SUBTOTAL	$2,762.
		Outstanding	1,247.00	Outstanding	500.
TOTAL	$9,078.44	TOTAL	$5,254.50	TOTAL	$3,262.
NET PROFIT	$4,730.38	NET PROFIT	$325.59	NET PROFIT	$1,384.

Projected Expense and Income for Historical Housewalk

	INCOME	EXPENSES
Tickets 3,000 @ $3.50	$10,500	
Advertising	3,000	
Boutique	1,000	
Country store	1,000	
	$15,500	
Promotion — photographer, entertaining		$800
Refreshments (50¢ per person)		1,500
Printing and paper		
Tickets — donated		
Posters and post cards		90
Program		500
Postage — 10,000 postcards		200
Gifts to hostesses		50
Policemen		180
		$3,320
Projected Profit		$12,180

Chapter 22

INVOLVING THE POWER STRUCTURE

WHY involve people in the power structure? Traditionally, the community agencies serving mentally retarded and physically handicapped people were begun by parents of handicapped children. Oftentimes, the boards of directors of these agencies, as well as other social service agencies, do not have strong representation of the power structure in the community. Colleges and hospitals, on the other hand, have significant representation of the power structure on their boards. Social service agencies cop out by maintaining that influential people do not want to be identified with social problems.

In the field of social services, it is deemed appropriate to have the board of directors or policy-making board of the agency be representative of the broad community, as well as both sides of the social service being provided — consumer and professional. Therefore, the policy-making board might be comprised of one-third consumers and/or consumer representatives, one-third professionals, and one-third influential citizens. The consumers know what the problems they experience are, the professionals know remedies, and the influential citizens know how to use community resources to implement the programs recommended by professionals.

For policy-making purposes, this is a viable board makeup. For social action purposes, including social change and fund raising, it is less ideal. The board is slanted toward a specific problem with limited general community input. The social problem being addressed involves the reverse ratio. The consumers and their families compromise perhaps one twentieth to one tenth of the population.[1]

---

[1]Study indentifying the incidence of handicapped people in DuPage County (pop. 276,000) revealted 7.7 percent of families reported having a handicapped member. R. Nelson. Ray Graham Association for the Handicapped, 1976.

The social action required to integrate handicapped people into the community, therefore, necessitates developing a number of additional options for community involvement. A volunteer league with broad membership in the community and the board president sitting on the agency's policy-making board is one solution. A board makeup of one-half consumers and consumer representatives, either family members or persons employed as professional staff in the human service delivery system, with the other half interested citizens is another possibility. The citizens might represent all economic and social strata which leaves the number of board positions available for influential citizens very limited.

The formation of a board of trustees for the existing agency or a separate support organization (a foundation) would offer a vehicle for the involvement of the power structure in the social service agency. The broadly based board of directors can concern itself with ongoing policy decisions and the board of trustees or foundation can concern itself with long-range planning and mobilizing resources.

The board of trustees and foundation concepts permit legitimation of the cause among the influential people and the power structure in the community. The separate foundation simultaneously solves the problem of establishing a constituency to raise money for capital purposes, as well as establishing a holding corporation for assets which can then be leased to the direct service agency (see Chapter 23).

Sociologists John B. Mitchell and Sheldon G. Lowry[2] maintain that successful social action proceeds through relatively well-defined steps, involves community leaders, and takes into account the power structure of that particular community. The movement of handicapped people into the mainstream of life is facilitated smoothly and without resort to militancy if the agencies actively involve influential and decision-making members of the community in establishing programs. Their support will greatly facilitate the evolution of medical services,

---

[2]J. B. Mitchell and G. S. Lowry, *Power Structure, Community Leadership and Social Action,* North Central Regional Extension Publication No. 35; reprinted in *The Grantsman,* Spring 1974.

developmental opportunities, facilities, necessary zoning changes, and eliminate many levels of discrimination. First, by virtue of their position in the community, the influentials and decision makers are able to establish a welcoming climate at the upper level of community functioning. Secondly, because they are in the best position to generate substantial sums of voluntary dollars, programs can be started and buildings and capital purchased totally independent of tax dollars.

The process of fund raising is simply another step in the legitimation process in the community. Broad community education and fund raising are essential to acceptance at all economic and social levels. However, the single most powerful group in the community is often comprised of a small number of decision makers and influential or long-time wealthy residents.

Terry Clark[3] in *Community Structure and Decision Making* defines power as "the capacity to mobilize resources for the accomplishment of intended effects with recourse to the same type of sanctions to encourage compliance."

Robert Presthus[4] conceptualizes elites as a minority of specialized leaders who enjoy disproportionate amounts of power in community affairs. He refers to the two elites — political and economic.

Presthus's research indicates that although economic elites deny prestige to local political figures, most ordinary citizens respect local officeholders. The most visible or "best known" leaders, as perceived by the broad community, may actually be lieutenants or "leg men."

Presthus conceptualizes power as a system of social relationships.

> One is that individual power is always worked out within some larger framework or institutional power. Even Robinson Crusoe's relations with Friday faced this imperative. Men are powerful in relation to other men. The

[3]T. N. Clark, *Community Structure and Decision Making: Comparative Analysis* (Scranton, Pennsylvania, Chandler Publishing Co., 1968).

[4]R. Presthus, *Men at the Top: A Study in Community Power* (Fair Lawn, New Jersey, Oxford University Press, 1962), p. 210.

> other fact is that the power of any given individual is in large measure a result of his ability to manipulate this larger system. This presupposes in every community a certain ongoing network of fairly stable subsystems, activated by social, economic, ethnic, religious, and friendship ties and claims. Such systems of interest, values, and power have desirable consequences for their members to the extent that they satisfy various human needs. In a sense, however, such subsystems are suprahuman, in that they tend to persist indefinitely and, more important, that their members may change but the underlying network of interrelated interests and power relations continues.

In describing the decision-making process in communities, Presthus says:

> Modern democratic societies are generally believed to be pluralistic to the extent that governmental power and influence over important public decisions are broadly shared with a great number of private organizations. Many of these organizations are "extra-official." They have neither legal nor constitutional status, but instead exercise their influence on government informally. Using many paths of access, they apply pressure in an attempt to shape proposed actions to their own design. Obviously, no group succeeds in achieving its preferences all the time, nor are all groups equally concerned with all issues. Instead, each bargains and marshals its resources to do battle on those issues that impinge upon its own interests. A myriad of tactics is used in such struggles, including exchange, in which one group supports another on one issue, in return for which it receives support on another issue of vital importance to itself.

The political power structure starts with the chairman of both or all political parties. The party having the most voters also has the most influential party chairman. Not necessarily because that chairman is the best leader, but because he "chairs" the most voters. Political influentials enjoy power of a more transient nature than "economic" influentials because the political power is subject to the election process. Economic based power, therefore, frequently transcends political power. Because it is not as subject to being withdrawn it is more stable.

Individuals or groups with significant wealth can always arrange to have their views heard and fostered regardless of the political party in power at the moment.

Sociologists John B. Mitchell of Ohio State University and Sheldon Lowry of Michigan State University,[5] wrote an excellent synopsis describing power structures, community leadership, and social action. They outline social action stages and community leadership as follows.

> Influentials have the greatest amount of power (see Figure 1). While one of their primary functions is legitimation, they generally are very knowledgeable and should be looked to for ideas and information. Lieutenants are in the second echelon

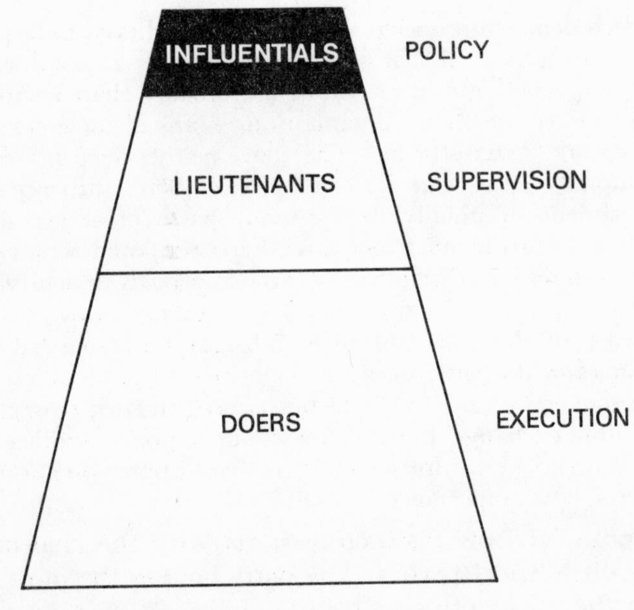

Figure 1.

[5] J. B. Mitchell, S. G. Lowry. *Power Structure, Community Leadership and Social Action,* North Central Regional Extension Publication No. 35, reprinted in *The Grantsman,* Spring 1974.

of power. Their primary function is the supervision and implementation of policy. They generally are closely associated with influentials. Doers are community leaders at the third level of power. They are sometimes referred to as "leg men" because their primary function is to carry out decisions.

Every community is unique and has its own variation of these general types.

Social Action Stages and Community Leadership

Stages of Community Action	Levels of Leadership Involved
1. Inception of the idea (problem or need)	May be a mixture, but primarily influentials and lieutenants.
2. Legitimation	Influentials.
3. Creating general awareness of problem or need	Lieutenants and doers working with a special committee and perhaps with other organizations.
4. Determining the goals (plan of action)	Lieutenants and doers working with local organizations.
5. Mobilization for action and implementation	Lieutenants for supervision and liaison, doers for action, and selected influentials for symbolic acts such as the "ground breaking ceremony" and cutting the ribbon on opening day.
6. Evaluation	Persons most involved in the project, especially professional change agents.

They describe the types of power structure as (1) pyramidal — characterized by a small number of persons at top, (2) factional — two or more factions that compete in the arena of community life, (3) coalitional — influentials from various power loci form temporary coalition, and (4) amorphus — no discernible pattern of power is evident.[6]

Pyramidal Power Structures

The pyramidal power structure is characterized by a small number of persons at the top. Therefore, it often is referred to as a concentrated power structure. The major control over resources and employment lies in the hands of one family, one industry, or one tightly knit clique. In some instances, the industry is owned by the dominant family, so resources and power are controlled by the same persons. Especially in small communities, a whole range of major local issues may be dealt with by the dominant family, by management of the only industry, or by a small, closely knit clique. The same individuals usually are influential in all major community decisions and projects.

In the case of a family-dominated community, positions of power tend to be inherited and, therefore, held for many years. In a one-industry town, the formal power structure of the industry carries over into community affairs. The executives of the company become very influential in the community.

One well-known study described an extended family that dominated much of the economic life of a medium-sized city. Five brothers settled in this community at the turn of the century. Later, as their sons and daughters married, many of them remained in the city.

This family developed a prosperous industry and participated in many facets of community life. The family owned a bank, members served on various boards of directors,

---

[6]J. B. Mitchell and S. G. Lowry.

and they took an interest in community agencies. Members of this family became very influential in the life of the community. They had to be reckoned with in any major undertaking in this city.

Clique

When power alignments take the form of a closely knit clique which constitutes the primary policy-making structure of the community, these individuals come from the top levels of power in the dominant social systems in the community. The most frequently represented systems are business and industry, plus some professionals and representatives of local government.

In one small community the "invisible government" was composed of three men — a feed dealer, a lawyer, and the newspaper editor. The leadership roles of these men were apparent in virtually all important community issues. Even in rural areas power is likely to be vested primarily in those who run the local town or village "Main Street" businesses and, in some instances, lawyers and those who control mass media such as newspaper editors. When farmers are represented in the power structure, they usually are individuals who control large resources and come from families with a past history of high social standing in the community.

In small communities, power and social class are likely to go hand-in-hand. A general fusing of the political, economic, and educational systems may also take place. These persons may be referred to in local terminology as "the elites," "best families," the "upper crust," or similar titles.

In view of present community changes and future trends, the one clique, one family, or one industry type of power structure can be expected to decline in prevalence and importance. With increased diversity and more outside forces affecting communities, the power alignments will involve more people and be more pluralistic.

A broadening of the power base can be expected in most

communities as industrialization continues, accompanied by the increasing influence of forces from outside the local community. The established influentials will have to share power and decision making with the more recent arrivals — such as executives of newly located industrial plants.

In the more complex industrialized and urbanized communities, many community influentials are more specialized. That is, these persons tend to devote their time and energy to only certain kinds of issues rather than the whole gamut of community problems.

Factional

This form of community power alignment is characterized by two or more factions (sometimes referred to as special interest groups, pressure groups, or power blocks) that compete with or actively oppose each other in the arena of community life. A

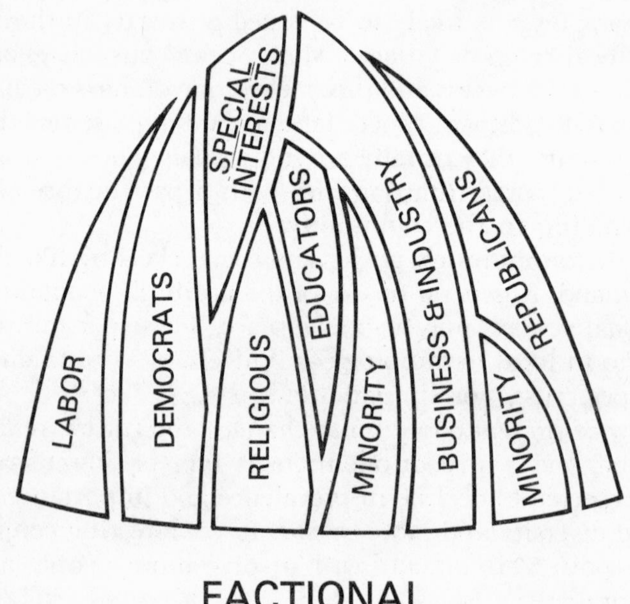

Figure 2.

good example is a community where the two major political parties are of relatively equal strength. Each party is organized and competes with the other for various resources and rewards within the community.

Industry and labor represent a factional power structure in some communities. In others, professional politicians, sometimes backed by ethnic or minority groups, largely control the local government while the economic, industrial, and professional sector stands in opposition through its trade and community service organizations. The latter often are identified as "Economic Dominants" or "The Establishment."

Of more recent origin are factions representing such groups as disadvantaged citizens forming organizations and competing for control and allocation of community resources and facilities.

Coalitional

The basic notion portrayed in this type of power structure is that influentials from various loci of power from a temporary coalition with regard to key community projects in which they are interested. The membership of such coalitions varies from project to project, and once a project is completed, the coalition is dissolved. Hence, these groups often are referred to as fluid coalitions.

These arrangements represent a pluralistic (diversified) type of community power structure. They involve a sizable number of able people who address themselves to particular projects or issues. Usually these individuals are not involved in a large number of projects or issues.

While these influentials can and sometimes do act in concert on community projects, they ususally are selective in their involvement. Some individuals have more interest in and, therefore, become more involved in certain issues than in others. However, all of these individuals have considerable power in the community.

Two characteristics differentiate the faction from the coalitional: (1) the factions endure for long periods of time, i.e., the same organizations and positions are important year after year, while coalitions are formed and then dissolved as projects are completed; (2) factions address themselves to a variety of community issues, projects, and programs, wheras the coalitions are more likely to participate in particular projects.

One of the best known research efforts on the coalition power structure utilized what is known as "the issue approach" to determine the power arrangement in a city. Leadership patterns in three major areas were studied — urban redevelopment, public education, and political nominations. One of the major conclusions from this study was that a leader in one issue or project is not likely to be involved in a second or third project.

Similar findings were reported from a study of a small town. The researcher found that no one person or group exerted leadership in all areas of community life. He found leadership to be a pluralistic phenomenon. Where an overlap in the leadership in different projects occurred, the persons involved were public officials such as the city manager, mayor, and members of the city council.

These studies and others point out the prevalence of small groupings of influential people who have considerable power in their communities. The number of influentials who are concerned with multiple issues varies. In general, influentials are selective about the projects in which they become involved.

Amorphous

Amorphous is the term which is applied to a community where no discernible or persistent pattern of power is evident. The leadership situation is shapeless, for no cleavages or structures seem to be functioning.

This type of situation does not occur very frequently. In a survey of sixty-one studies of community power, only seven reported an amorphous power situation.

The economic-based influentials are frequently those people who settled the area and own considerable assets in the community or those who control the economic well-being of the community — farm, factory, stores, banks, etc. — by providing employment. Influential people may not be as highly visible as decision makers. The decision makers, however, traditionally respond positively to the recommendations of the influentials.

All the members of each board are not real decision makers. As in any social structure, a few members of each board dominate and others follow.

Comparing the well-established, wealthy family names with those names which overlap on the hospital board, college board, country club, bank boards, and corporate boards will usually reveal the true "influentials." Those names which overlap on the other boards are readily identifiable as decision makers. Decision makers may be wealthy because of inherited wealth, affluent because of their own earning power, or of relatively modest means. Union leaders are influentials.

In a rural area, the influential people are generally the largest landholders, perhaps farmers, or the owner of the major income producing enterprise in town — coal mine, granary, ranch, etc. In some cases, the person who controls the economic well-being of the community may be an absentee owner who resides elsewhere. This is as true in a rural area as in the inner city of a major metropolitan area. This "influential" should definitely be included in the legitimation process — even though he does not live in the immediate area. In a community where a large residential institution for handicapped people employs most of the people in the town, the economic influential could be either the state or the employees' union.

In a metropolitan area, undoubtedly a plethora of agencies will be serving disabled individuals. Hopefully geographic boundaries play some part in determining service area. The defined service area should be the "community" to be organized and developed for each agency. The influential people approached should have particular relevance to that specific geographical area. Since the need for services is most critical and widespread in the lower socio-economic areas, people in top management of a corporation which controls a considerable number of economic livelihoods are also probably not residents of the local community. However, if the corporation is located there, an influential is needed to effect the changes,

WHO HAS ACCESS TO WHOM

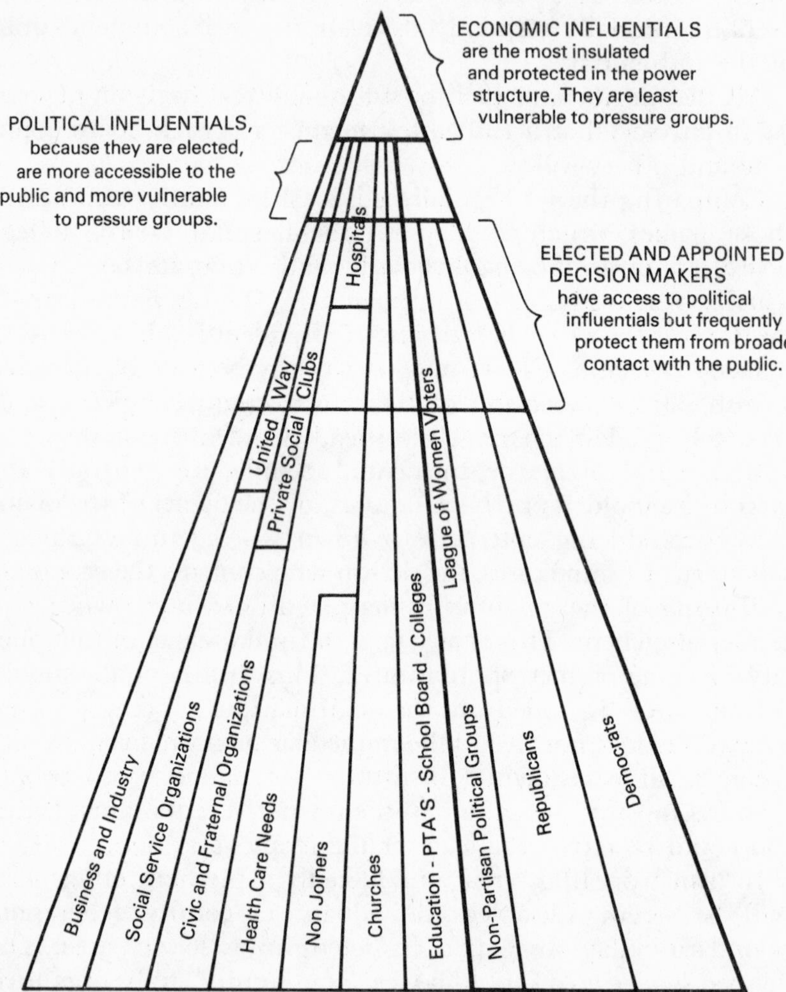

IN A SAMPLE COMMUNITY

- Some people belong to many groups.
- Many people belong to more than one group.
- Most people belong to at least one group.
- People flow in and out of interest groups as their needs and roles change.

Figure 3.

implement the program, or build the facility and should be approached for assistance in organizing other influential support. Union officials are certainly influential people — they control the economic well-being of multitudes of their members. Politicians who control patronage jobs are influential for the same reason.

The power structure in a metropolitan area is usually extremely complex and multilayered, with numerous individuals and interest groups having the right and ability to take part in a decision-making process. Community leaders vary in the amount and type of power of influence they possess and the kinds of functions they perform.

Influential people make good members of boards of directors, trustees, etc. because they can influence decision makers. It is often difficult for elected officials and many decision makers to be on the board of directors of an extracurricular organization because they are subject to conflict of interest charges when a decision they make as a board member affects their primary interest area.

On leadership, Etzioni says, "An individual whose power is chiefly derived from his organizational position is referred to as an official. An individual whose ability to control others is chiefly personal is referred to as an informal leader. One who commands both positional and personal power is a formal leader."[7]

Robert F. Bales, group analysis specialist, normally develops not one but two leaders — a task leader and a social leader. The function of the first is to keep everybody on the problem. The function of the second is to keep them in good temper.

A change agent must recognize the social action process as a series of stages from inception through legitimation, creating awareness, determining goals, mobilizing resources, action, and evaluation. Understanding who the community leaders are, what their sphere of influence is, and at what point in the process they can be most potent is basic to creating change. A clear understanding of community power and leadership is required to insure adequate consideration of community issues.

---

[7]A. Etzioni, Modern Organizations (Englewood Cliffs, New Jersey, Prentice-Hall, Inc., 1964), p. 61.

Chapter 23

DEVELOPMENT OF AN EFFECTIVE MEMBERSHIP OR ANNUAL GIVING CAMPAIGN

PEOPLE respond to their peers. The more respected a volunteer is within his peer group and below his peer group, the more responsive his peers will be to his solicitation for help or financial support.

1. Assign a staff member to design and direct the campaign.
2. Have a board committee select a campaign chairman capable of commanding respect, motivating contributors and volunteers. Establish a timetable and a goal in dollars for the campaign and stick to it.
3. Make prospect cards for all past contributors and members indicating past history of contributions and identify new prospects with help of committee members.

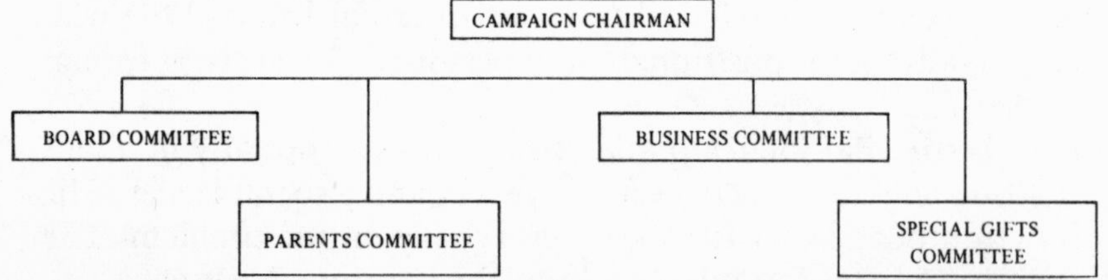

4. Have the committee chairman select committee members.
5. Hold motivational, information luncheon for all chairmen and committee members and press. Hire photographer.
   a. Explain the program.
   b. Explain the need for funds.
   c. Explain how each person can help.
   d. Give each person a campaign kit containing
      (1) Instructions for him and his other committee members.

(2) Materials needed by him for solicitation.

(3) Brochures, annual reports, sample letters, return envelopes.

(4) Appropriate prospect cards of past contributors.

6. Arrange individual committee meetings

a. *Board Committee* — Chairman should be an aggressive, respected board member. Ask each board member who is not on another committee to write 24, 50, or 100 letters to past supporters, as well as friends or acquaintances who have not contributed in the past. Ask each board member to call at least 10 friends after his letter is sent for follow-up.

b. *Parents' Committee* — Chairman should be an articulate parent, capable of motivating other parents. Have Parent Committee members hold meeting and write letters to all other parents, urging them to become members.

c. *Business Committee* — Chairman should be a prestigious individual in business locally or with good business contacts. Committee members should be invited by the chairmen — using approximately half businessmen who have had some involvement with the agency and half who are completely new to the scene. A committee of fifteen to twenty-five is a good number to start with. Arrange a luncheon at a good restaurant, convenient to the majority of the local business community. Ask each committee member to invite five to twenty other businessmen to hear about the agency and its ability to help handicapped people learn to help themselves. Attached are sample materials for Ray Graham's Business Campaign.

The Luncheon — Welcome by the Chairman of the Business Campaign. Introduction of Board President and Overall Membership Chairman. Have a good slide presentation of the agency's program presented by the agency's most articulate spokesman.

Have the executive director or appropriate staff member explain the financial situation briefly and clearly.

Have the Business Campaign Chairman announce the Business Committee's goal and explain the ways each person in attendance can help.

Have the Membership Chairmen identify the overall financial goals of the Membership Campaign.

All materials and presentations should be attractively and economically produced. Businessmen positively relate to successful ventures. The following are ingredients which contribute to success:

(1) A real need, well-expressed,
(2) An achievable goal,
(3) An attractively packaged venture — luncheon meeting, breakfast meeting — well written and produced materials,
(4) An identified way for each individual to help,
(5) The potential for success, enthusiastically expressed.

The following year, the Business Committee can expand and subdivide for recruitment into corporate committees — local businessmen, bankers, realtors, attorneys, etc. — and continue expanding until virtually every group is being reached in a personal way.

d. *Special Gifts Committee* — Chairman should be a well-respected member of the community capable of encouraging donations and motivating peers to solicit contributions.

The goal of this committee is to personally solicit gifts of $100 or more from affluent individuals and foundations.

The appropriate setting for a meeting might be the chairman's home or at a country club for lunch. A similar program presentation with slides and an explanation of the budget and financial need, as presented at the businessmen's luncheon, should be done for the committee members.

All past contributors of $100 or more, who are not

covered by the Business Committee, should be assigned to the Special Gifts Committee. Each past and potential special gifts contributor should receive a letter followed by a personal call. They can then either each choose 10 prospects to call upon or plan a similar large luncheon for 100 special gifts prospects and have a program designed to depict the need and motivate donations. Whether personal calls or a large luncheon is used as the form of contact, each committee member should be given specific people to "call on." Repeat givers should get the same personal attention in following years as in the first year.

Requests for substantial gifts might be made jointly by a staff member and peer group volunteer, if the volunteer does not feel his knowledge of the agency is adequate.

7. Arrange bimonthly luncheon or breakfast meetings with the Campaign Chairman and Committee Chairman together. Urge each Committee Chairman to hold regular "report" meetings with his committee members. Use the meetings as a forum to exchange ideas and permit each Committee Chairman to "show off" his achievements.

In all committees, you can expect one-third of the volunteers to be really terrific and produce even more than they were asked to, one-third of the volunteers to do just what they were asked to — with some prodding — and one-third of the volunteers to explain why they did not succeed or were unable to get to it. Have a final report meeting with the chairman scheduled two weeks before the final deadline and reassign the unfulfilled responsibilities of drop-outs.

Smile a lot at everyone. See that the people who really worked get appropriate recognition.

Despite most protestations of "I don't expect any special recognition, I did it because I wanted to," the vast majority of volunteers do appreciate public recognition and approval of their peers. The Campaign Chairman's most valuable activity is expressing his admiration for the volunteer's activities and achievements. There are always just a few truly outstanding volunteers and these should be recognized.

The atmosphere of the after campaign period is as important as the amount of money raised. If it has been a positive experience, the volunteers will be more than willing to work again on the next campaign. By building on past support, the base continues to broaden, the pyramid deepens, and the money multiplies. Remember, your goal is to continually build a larger, deeper faceted pyramid of support.

March 15, 1974

Dear ___________

Just two weeks ago today you very kindly gave your valuable time to hear and see our story. We sincerely appreciate your coming to our lunch and for spending this time.

You indicated that you were interested in placement of handicapped personnel. I wish to advise you that Mrs. Gaver will contact you regarding this if she has not already done so.

You will be kept informed as to our progress and hope to again have the opportunity to discuss the progress of Ray Graham Association for the Handicapped.

Cordially,

RAY GRAHAM ASSOCIATION FOR THE HANDICAPPED

515 Factory Road, Addison, Illinois 60101

Phone (312) 543-2440

__________ I am interested in employing handicapped people.
Have Mrs. Gaver call me.

__________ I am interested in having the Ray Graham Association bid on subcontract work. Have Mr. Johnson call me.

__________ I will write letters asking for contributions to the Ray Graham Association Scholarship fund. Have Mrs. Nelson call me.

__________ I would like to be a member of the Ray Graham Scholarship Club.
I will underwrite a Ray Graham Scholarship in the amount of:

__________ $600 Full Year
__________ $300 Half Year
__________ $100 Two Months

NAME ____

COMPANY ____

ADDRESS ______________________________ TOWN __________

TELEPHONE ____

January 31, 1974

Dear Committee Member:

We have established the date and place for the "Business Friends of Ray Graham" luncheon as March 1st, 12 noon at Sharko's Restaurant in Villa Park.

We would appreciate having you send carbon copies of letters of invitation or a list of names of those people invited to Mrs. Nelson at the Association Office.

Please accept my warmest personal thanks for helping.

Sincerely,

T. L. Harrigan
Board President

Dear

DuPage County has an estimated 15,000 handicapped residents.

We are organizing a special luncheon for prominent members of the West Suburban business community. We would like to ask for your advice and assistance in helping Ray Graham Association to:

1. Obtain the subcontract work to be performed by Ray Graham's workshops.
2. Stimulate employment opportunities for handicapped people.
3. Organize an annual scholarship campaign to assure educational and vocational training opportunities for local handicapped residents.

Will you join us for lunch on February __________ at __________ at ________________ ?

I'll call you next week.

Chapter 24

A BLUEPRINT FOR ORGANIZING A BOARD OF TRUSTEES OR A SEPARATE SUPPORT FOUNDATION

FIRST, have the agency board of directors determine whether it wants a board of trustees or a separate support foundation. In order to attract and involve influential people in a meaningful way to achieve the integration of handicapped people into the mainstream of community life, the agency must identify an appropriate and meaningful role for the community's influential citizens. The trustee or foundation board role is a familiar one to the influential person and since most direct service agencies can use additional financial support, as well as pure prestige or influence, these two structures lend themselves well to involving the power structure in the community in helping disabled individuals to develop to their maximum.

Identify the most respected, influential, and wealthy members of the community. Single out the most approachable person in this group. Explain the service your agency performs, the needs that are still unmet, and the necessity of his involvement to the future of handicapped people.

The selection and motivation of the appropriate person is of prime importance. Learn as much about your object of concern as possible. If you do not know the individual, have a mutual friend introduce you. Make an appointment to see him. Explain why it is necessary to expand the voluntary contributions. Invite him to see your program. Be prepared to answer critical questions on your budget and management. Be scrupulously honest.

Redefine why you need this specific person to help you recruit other influential people or "substantial members of the community." Ask him to suggest others for a board of trustees or foundation board, whose purpose is to generate contributions.

Submit the names you have collected for membership. Among the names should be at least one of each of the following kinds of individuals:

1. Prominent businessman or businesswoman
2. A prominent, independently wealthy man
3. A prominent, independently wealthy woman
4. A well-respected attorney
5. A well-known affluent individual known for his special charisma
6. A well-known "society" woman

Have a small luncheon for this group by your "leader." Give a good, solid presentation on what your agency does, what it needs, how that will help handicapped people, why you need the help of each person in the room, and why you need a board of trustees or a foundation.

Announce the next luncheon or breakfast meeting. Hold it at the program site. Explain the program, the agency, and the unmet needs again. Ask for their suggestions. Establish a first year goal.

The first year's activities should have specific goals:

1. Organize a specific number of trustees.
2. Hold monthly executive committee meetings.
3. Hold quarterly total board meetings.
4. Hold monthly individual committee meetings:
   a. Establish a membership committee to expand the board.
   b. Establish an organization committee — if a separate support foundation is to be established, an attorney should be chairman to prepare the incorporation documents and establish the relationship of the two boards.
   c. Publicize the founding members and the organizational activities.
   d. Hold first election of officers.
   e. Establish a fund-raising committee to define next year's goal and method of fund raising.

Since this is an embryonic organization, the first year of operations will be directed toward organization, make the first year's dollar goal one which is easily achievable. The first year will be spent educating directors and trustees regarding needs and helping them identify their goals. It is crucial that the staff person assigned to work with the trustees accept their input graciously. While the staff can direct and lead toward specific goals, the trustees themselves must feel they have chosen the direction in which they are going. Commitment to a goal is the result of having taken part in the establishment of that goal. This cannot be accomplished in a few days or weeks. Once the trustees accept a commitment of their own choosing as a group, they will be most likely to execute the action necessary to achieve their established goal.

Chapter 25

CRITERIA FOR THE DEVELOPMENT OF A SUPPORT FOUNDATION

IF there is a conflict in having a direct service agency own property because funding sources such as state grant-in-aid monies are not applicable on mortgage payments for the acquisition of real property or equipment, it might be worth considering forming a nonprofit, tax exempt holding corporation.

The advantages of a nonprofit, tax exempt holding corporation are fairly obvious:

1. When buildings required by the direct service agency must be substantially modified to operate the program, the cost of modifications represents a major investment which should be protected either through a long-term lease or ownership.
2. The ownership of assets by the holding corporation improves the credit rating of both the direct service agency and the holding corporation.
3. The growth and protection of capital can positively affect the ability of the direct service agency to continually provide improved and expanded services as they are needed.
4. The function of acquiring and investing capital funds to more adequately meet clients' programmatic needs offers a positive way to involve influential members of the community in becoming aware of the need for the agency's services and the needs of the people it serves.
5. Any monies which might flow through as profits from a not-for-profit organization to a for-profit entrepreneur can be retained in the service delivery system to directly benefit the people served by the agency.

A holding corporation for a direct service agency should be

organized as a support organization, as explained in 509A3 in the IRS code. The support organization must prove it is "substantially controlled" by a 501C3 organization.

Any direct service agency receiving the majority of its income from tax sources would unequivocably qualify as a 501C3 organization. A holding corporation which was organized as a free standing 501C3 organization would have great difficulty maintaining its public charity status if its chief source of income is voluntary contributions.

	Income	*Portion which is nonpublic*	*Portion which is public*
Contribution from Mrs. Glos	$15,000	$14,000	$1,000
Contribution from Mr. Butler	$15,000	$14,000	$1,000
Contribution from Mr. Bates	$10,000	$ 9,000	$1,000
Benefit tickets $25 a person			
Net income from benefit ($12.50 of each ticket is considered an exchange for services, the remaining $12.50 is treated as a contribution.)	$ 7,000	$ 3,500	$3,500
Two contributions of $1,000 each	$ 2,000		$2,000
Contributions under $1,000	$ 1,000		$1,000
	$50,000	$40,500	$9,500

IRS defines a public charity, as opposed to a private foundation, as one in which contributions from a single individual or corporation cannot exceed 2 percent of its total income that year. Therefore, with total income of $50,000 any gift over $1,000 is at least partially nonpublic. IRS requires that one-third of an organization's income be public, in this example at least $16,666 of the $50,000 must be public. Since only $9,500 qualified as public income, our example does not meet the IRS test. There are several other levels of tests applicable but this is the most stringent. The reason these limitations have been set was to eliminate many of the abuses practiced by some private foundations.

If an organization loses its public charity status, it can still retain its tax exempt status but is reclassified as a private foundation. Hundreds of pages of rules apply to private foundations, but the major disadvantage of a private foundation, versus a public charity or support foundation, is that the donor cannot claim the appreciated value of a gift to a private foundation and can claim the appreciated value of a gift to a public charity.

Therefore, if the intention in organizing a holding corporation is to acquire property and large contributions, it is wise to consider the organizational structure which embodies all the advantages of a public charity to make giving as attractive as possible to the potential donor. This would be the 509A3.

IRS defines a 509A3 or support organization as one which is organized exclusively for the support of one or more specifically stated charities. In effect, the 509A3 is so closely tied to the public charity that the 509A3 organization can "lean" on the status of the 509A1 organization. A direct service agency would always be a 501C3 organization since its income is predominately from tax dollars which are all "public" monies. If the holding corporation is organized as a support organization which is closely tied to the above type of agency, then the problem of accepting sizeable voluntary contributions is no longer present. A hypothetical example would be the following.

ABC AGENCY BUDGET

$200,000

Income	*Income*	*Public Income*	*Non-public Income*
DMH Grant	$100,000	$100,000	
Income from School Districts	50,000	50,000	
Parent Fees	10,000		$10,000
Revenue Sharing or Community Fund Support	40,000	40,000	
		$190,000	$10,000

The 509A3 support organization or holding corporation for

the ABC Agency could then accept as many as three $100,000 contributions or even one $300,000 contribution from an individual without endangering the public charity status, i.e. the direct service agency's public income of $190,000 permits up to $570,000 in large contributions to be accepted by the direct service agency or its support foundation in one fiscal year without endangering the public charity status of either the direct service agency or the support foundation.

"Substantial control" of the support organization by the direct service agency is the key to retaining 509A3 public charity status. The articles of incorporation for the holding corporation must be written to state their purpose as being "solely for the support of __________ Corporation." The most conservative interpretation of this would mean that the board of directors of the direct service agency elects a majority of the directors of the holding corporation. Following is an example of the election process in Ray Graham Association and the Foundation for the Handicapped, its 509A3 organization.

ELECTION OF BOARDS

Ray Graham Association	*Foundation for the Handicapped*
Board of directors elected at annual meeting in March by membership of Ray Graham.	8 directors elected by the Ray Graham Board.
The Ray Graham directors elect the Ray Graham officers.	7 directors elected by foundation trustees at foundation annual meeting in September.
	Directors meet monthly.
	Trustees meet quarterly.
	Foundation directors elected by Ray Graham Board.
	Foundation directors elected by foundation trustees.
Executive director should sit on support organization board to coordinate policy.	Director of Development should sit on support organization board to coordinate fund raising.

Advantages of Separate Holding Corporation	*As a Separate Public Charity 509A1*	*As a Support Organization 509A3*
State funds given to direct serving agency can be used by making rental payments to holding corporation to pay off mortgage.	Holding corporation has maximum freedom of operation.	Direct service organization has guarantee of control of disposition of assets.
Additional citizen involvement is possible as directors and trustees of holding corporations.	Same.	Same.
The special skills of "influentials" can be utilized in a meaningful way by assigning them the task as directors and trustees to protect and wisely invest capital assets.	For the whole community or numerous agencies.	For specifically named agency or agencies.
Funds flowing through the holding corporation in the form of rent can be kept in use for expanding programs for handicapped people rather than providing profit for a private entrepreneur.	For the whole community or numerous agencies.	For specifically named agency or agencies.
	(DISADVANTAGE)	(MAJOR ADVANTAGE)
	Contributions must be carefully spaced out to avoid losing public charity status and to be classified as a private foundation.	Large contributions can come in at the donor's convenience because of expanded income base of public charity and support organization.

A support foundation can also be created and operated for the support of a public taxing body such as a department of public health or a mental health clinic. Frequently a public health department could not own a building unless it was totally paid for. A support foundation which is a separate legal entity can own the building and receive rent from the health department to pay the mortgage and water. Finally, competent legal and tax counsel should be used in forming these organizations to adapt them to local and state statutes.

SECTION VI
Summary

Chapter 26

SUMMARY OF CONSIDERATIONS IN CREATING ACCEPTANCE IN THE COMMUNITY FOR HANDICAPPED PEOPLE

Liberty

> We the people of the United States, in order to form a more perfect union, establish justice, insure domestic tranquility, provide for the common defense, promote the general welfare and secure the blessings of liberty to ourselves and our posterity, do ordain and establish this Constitution for the United States of America.

Preamble to the United States Constitution

Equality

> All persons born or naturalized in the United Sates and subject to the jurisdiction thereof, are citizens of the United States and of the State wherein they reside. No State shall make or enforce any law which shall abridge the privileges or immunities of citizens of the United States; nor shall any State deprive any person of life, liberty or property without due process of law; nor deny to any person within its jurisdiction the equal protection of the laws.

Amendment Fourteen of the United States Constitution

The Rights of the Individual versus
The Rights of Society

Equal protection of the laws refers to both the individual and the rest of society. Each individual has freedom of choice as long as he conforms to the law. If the law is not just, it should be changed. If an individual has repeatedly exhibited behavior dangerous to others, society has the right to be protected from that person. The judgment that a person poses a threat to society must be made with great care for it deprives that person of a great degree of freedom.

Private Property

The United States economic and legal systems are built on the basis of the right to own private property. Most families in the United States own their home and it is their major financial asset. Any threat to the value of that asset would for many individuals be of major importance.

The Fourteenth Amendment has been used many times in Supreme Court decisions to protect persons and corporations from arbitrary state action that would enfringe upon either personal or property rights.

Needs versus Values

In keeping with Abraham Maslow's concept of a hierarchy of needs, expressed in terms of a triangle, the most basic needs relate to survival. The base of the triangle is the satisfaction of physiological drives and then the protection of security needs, followed by social and ego needs for many people. Therefore, one's belief or value system satisfies ego and social needs. The value system is operative only as long as it is not in conflict with lower order needs. Educate and involve others to eliminate fear and perceived conflict. Help the general public meet their social and ego needs by helping handicapped people.

Trust and Reliability

Every community has leaders and members whom others trust. The leaders and members must be educated to the need, involved in the change process, and then put in responsible positions to affect action. To whom will they listen? What do they suggest? The plan will vary, for every community is unique. Educate but listen.

The Nature of Helping

"It is one of the most beautiful compensations of life that no man can sincerely try to help another without helping himself."

Ralph Waldo Emerson

Attitudes

People with certain characteristics are discomforting to the dominant culture which views those qualities as different and therefore incompatible. When the characteristics of a particular group present a perceived threat to physical safety or economic security, negative attitudes may create real resistance to integration. Education can replace misinformation and misperceptions with more factual information on which to make decisions. However, actual involvement and experience with the stigmatized population will be required to really change attitudes and prejudices. Real involvement takes place through experience. Real experience comes from interacting with one another.

Communication

There must be both a sender and receiver in communicating. The message must be received, understood, and accepted for communication to occur. Flag waving and militancy may meet the ego needs of those who demand and demonstrate, but those tactics frequently create other barriers and in the end the people who were meant to be served suffer from the backlash. Gentle, firm insistence to back up the belief that handicapped people have the right to live in the mainstream of life, offered by a respected responsible group of local citizens, can insure that right. And finally, legal advocacy invoked when needed, most ideally carried through by respected members of the local community.

Acceptance

Acceptance can be encouraged, but true acceptance of one person by another can only be given voluntarily. It cannot be extracted or imposed. It is a gift from one being to another. Some people call it love.

Conclusion

The resources needed to create acceptance for handicapped people at the community level are: *Professional manpower* who *create the tools* and direct the means for creating change via education and involvement of *the power structure* and *the broad community* which then provides *the philosophical and financial support* to implement the change not only in their own behavior and attitudes, but to broaden the opportunity for disabled people.

The technology and professionalism which has developed to teach disabled person how to cope with society must also teach society how to cope with and accept people who are different.

It is not enough to merely teach disabled people how to function; we must remove the handicapping conditions which prevent them from living fully. We must accept the challenge of directing resources to change negative attitudes in professionals, decision makers, and the general public. We must remove the restrictions which inhibit disabled people from living as productively, independently, and with as much liberty as possible. Liberty and justice for all applies to lifestyle; it is not merely an ideological concept. Let us use sociologist Dr. John Koval's criteria for measuring our civilization. How good is the quality of life, how joyful are our people?

In 1968, William Saroyan wrote a Christmas message which might serve as an inspiration to all who place high value on the joy of life, but who are not content with the world as it is:

> In the time of your life, live — so that in that good time
> there shall be no ugliness or death for yourself or for any life

> your life touches. Seek goodness everywhere, and when it is found, bring it out of its hiding place and let it be free and unashamed. Place in matter and in flesh the least of the values, for these are the things that hold death and must pass away. Discover in all things that which shines and is beyond corruption. Encourage virtue in whatever heart it may have been driven into secrecy and sorrow by the shame and terror of the world. Ignore the obvious, for it is unworthy of the clear eye and the kindly heart. Be the inferior of no man, nor of any man be the superior. Remember that every man is a variation of yourself. No man's guilt is not yours, nor is any man's innocence a thing apart. Despise evil and ungodliness, but not men of ungodliness or evil. These, understand. Have no shame in being kindly and gentle, but if the time comes in the time of your life to kill the killers, kill and have no regret. In the time of your life, live — so that in that wondrous time you shall not add to the misery and sorrow of the world, but shall smile to the infinite delight and mystery of it.

If our society and its resources can help the quadraplegic operate a wheel chair by the breath from her mouth, if severely retarded persons with special training can outproduce a non-handicapped person on an assembly line, if an epileptic young girl can set a new record for long distance running, then our society can use its resources to change itself. Impossible, after all, is only a degree of difficulty. That which was impossible yesterday is merely subject to today's challenge.

Appendix

SELECTED READINGS

ADOPT Training Process. Developed by Fredric H. Margolis, FM Associates Ltd., Rockville, Maryland.

Analyzing Performance Problems or You Really Oughta Wanna. By Robert F. Mager and Peter Pipe, Fearon Publishers/Lear Siegler Inc., Educational Division, Belmont, California, 1970.

Child Care Volunteers Orientation. Citizens Planning Council, Voluntary Action Center, Rochester, New York.

A Handbook of Structured Experiences for Human Relations Training. Edited by J. William Pfeiffer and John E. Jones, University Associates, Publishers and Consultants, LaJolla, California.

Helping Skills: A Basic Training Program (A Leader's Manual and Trainees' Workbook). By Steven J. Danish and Allen L. Hauer, Behavioral Publications, New York, 1973.

An Irreverent Course in Writing Definitive Objectives. FM Associates Ltd., Rockville, Maryland.

Looking Into Leadership — Executive Libary. Leadership Resources Inc., Publications Division, Washington, D.C., 1966.

Looking Into Leadership Series. Leadership Resources Inc., Publications Division, Washington, D.C.

Preparing Instructional Objectives. By Robert F. Mager, Fearon Publishers Inc., Palo Alto, California, 1962.

Priorities in Adult Education. Edited by David B. Rauch, Publication of Adult Education Association, Macmillan Co., New York, 1972.

A Trainer's Guide to Andragogy: Its Concepts, Experiences and Application. By John D. Ingalls, United States Department of Health, Education and Welfare, Social and Rehabilitation Services, Washington, D.C., March 1972.

Training Objectives — A Participant-Oriented Approach. By Fredric H. Margolis, FM Associates Ltd., Rockville, Maryland, June 1970.

Training Student Volunteers. ACTION, National Student Volunteer Program, Washington, D.C.

Training Volunteer Leaders — A Handbook to Train Volunteers and Other Leaders of Program Groups, Research and Development Division, National Council of Young Men's Christian Associations, New York.

Twenty Exercises for Trainers. NTL Learning Resources Corp., Washington, D.C.

Your Volunteer Program. By Mary T. Swanson, EPDA Volunteer Coordinator's Program, Des Moines Area Community College, Ankeny, Iowa, April 1970.

BIBLIOGRAPHY

Accreditation Council for Facilities for the Mentally Retarded, Joint Commission on Accreditation of Hospitals: *Standards for Community Agencies Serving Persons with Mental Retardation and Other Developmental Disabilities.* Chicago Joint Commission on Accreditation of Hospitals, 1973.

Alinsky, Saul: *Revielle for Radicals.* New York, Random, 1969.

Argyris, Chris: *Personality and Organization.* New York, Har-Row, 1957.

Bell, A. H.: "Measure for adjustment of the physically disabled." *Psychological Reports, 21,* 1967.

Bengt, Nirje: *Reports on a Conference of Retarded Adults in Malmo,* mimeographed, 1968.

Benne, Kenneth and Birnbaum, Max: *Organizational Behavior and Administration,* rev. ed. Homewood, Illinois, Irwin, 1965.

Bremner, Robert H.: *American Philanthropy.* Chicago, U or Chicago Pr, 1960.

Brown, G.: Social factors influencing length of hospital stay of schizophrenic patients. *Br Med J, 2,* December 1959.

Browne, C. G.: Communication means understanding. In Davis, Keith and Scott, W. G.: *Readings in Human Relations.* New York, McGraw, 1959.

Conine, T. A.: Acceptance or rejection of disabled persons by teachers. *J Sch Health, 39,* 1969.

Conley, Ronald W.: *The Economics of Vocational Rehabilitation.* Baltimore, Maryland, Johns Hopkins, 1965.

Cooper, Q. B. and Early, D. F.: Evolution in the mental hospital: Review of a hospital population. *Br Med J,* June 1961.

Cox, Harvey: *The Feast of Fools.* New York, Har-Row, 1969.

Cross, K. W.: A survey of chronic patients in a mental hospital. *Br J Psychiatry,* January 1957.

Dybwad, Gunnar: Symposium on residential care.

The Gallup Organization: *Public Attitudes Regarding MR.* Princeton, New Jersey, President's Committee on Mental Retardation, December 3, 1973.

Gellman, William: *Rehabilitation Practices with the Physically Disabled.* New York, Columbia Union Pr, 1973.

Goffman, Erving: *Stigma: Notes on the Management of Spoiled Identity.* Englewood Cliffs, New Jersey, P-H, 1963.

Gottlieb, Jay and Siperstein, Gary: "Attitudes toward mentally retarded persons: Effect of attitude referent specificity." *Am J Ment Defic, 80* (4), 1976.

Harasymiw, Stefan J. and Horne, Marcia D.: Integration of handicapped children — its effect on teacher attitudes. *Education, 96* (2), Winter, 1975.

Harasymiw, Stefan J.; Horne, Marcia D.; and Lewis, Sally C.: *Attitude Congruence of Handicapped and Non-handicapped towards Disability Groups.* Paper presented at National Rehabilitation Association National Conference, Cincinnati, Ohio, October 15, 1975.

Harasymiw, Stefan J.; Horne, Marcia D.; Lewis, Sally C.; and Baron, Roberta: *Teacher and Pupil Disability Attitude Congruency.* Paper presented at the Annual International Exceptional Children Convention, Chicago, Illinois, April 1976.

Hebb, D. O.: On the nature of fear. *Psychol Rev, 53,* 1946.

Huizinga, John: *Homo Ludens: A Study of the Play Elements in Culture* (Trans by R. F. C. Hull). Boston, Massachusetts, Routledge & Kegan, 1949.

Illinois Department of Mental Health: *An Accountability Budget for Illinois Fiscal Year 1976-1977.* Springfield, Illinois, Office of the Controller, March 1976.

Illinois White House Conference: Workshop on housing. October 16-17, 1976.

Jacobs, Lewis: *The Movies as Medium.* Garden City, New York, Doubleday, 1970.

Johnson, Richard A.; Kast, Fremont E.; and Rosenzweig, James E.: Systems, theory and management. *Management Science,* January 1964.

Kendel, Denise and Williams, Richard: *Psychiatric Rehabilitation: Some Problems in Research.* New York, Atherton Press, 1964.

Knight, Arthur: *The Liveliest Art.* New York, NAL, 1971.

Koval, John P.: "Festivals." Lecture at DePaul University. Boston, Massachusetts, Routledge & Kegan, October 1976.

Kygel, R. B. and Wolfensberger, W. (Eds.): *Changing Patterns in Residential Services for the Mentally Retarded.* Washington, D.C., President's Committee on Mental Retardation, 1969.

LeUnes, Arnold; Christenson, Larry; and Wilkerson, Dennis: Institutional tour effects on attitudes related to mental retardation. *Am J Ment Defic, 79* (6), 1975.

Lewin, Kurt: *Principles of Topological Psychology.* New York, McGraw, 1966.

Ludwig, A. and Farrelly, F.: The code of chronicity. *Arch Gen Psychiatry,* December 15, 1966.

Mechanic, David: *Mental Health and Social Policy.* Englewood Cliffs, New Jersey, P-H, 1969.

National Association of Superintendents of Public Residential Facilities for the Mentally Retarded. 1974.

Natural History Magazine Supplement Special, December 1971.

Nelson, R.: *Public Policy for Habilitation and Rehabilitation Programs, "Human Profit vs. Material Profit."* Oak Brook, Illinois, Illinois Epilepsy Foundation, January 1977.

Nelson, R.: *Types of Housing Needed Based on Dupage County Survey of Needs.* Addison, Illinois, Ray Graham Association for the Handicapped, September 1976.

Pieper, Josef: *In Tune with the World.* New York, HarBraceJ, 1973.

Pierce, J. K.: *Symbols, Signals and Noise: The Nature and Process of Communication.* New York, Har-Row, 1961.

President's Committee on Mental Retardation: *Profiles of Community Residents for Retarded Children and Adults,* 1975.

President's Committee on Mental Retardation: *Mental Retardation Trend in State Services,* 1976.

Ray Graham Association for the Handicapped Annual Report 1975-76, Chicago, Illinois.

Ray Graham Association for the Handicapped 1975-76 Budget, Chicago, Illinois.

Scheerenberger, R. C.: A model for deinstitutionalization. *Ment Retard, 12* (6), December 1974.

Scheff, T.: Legitimate, transitional and illegitimate mental patients in a midwestern state. *Am J Psychiatry, 120,* September 1963.

Scott, W. G. and Mitchell, Terence R.: *Organization Theory: A Structure and Behavioral Analysis,* rev. ed. Homewood, Illinois, Irwin, 1976.

Shonty, F. C.: *The Psychological Aspects of Physical Illness and Disability.* New York, Macmillan, 1975.

Stedman, Donald J.: "Epilogue." In Paul, James L.; Wiegerink, Ron; and Newfeld, G. Ronald (eds.): *Advocacy: A Role for Developmental Disabilities Council,* 1974.

Tringo, J. L.: *The Hierarchy of Preference: A Comparison of Attitudes and Prejudice toward Specific Disability Groups.* Storrs, University of Connecticut, 1968.

Ullman, L. P.: *Institution and Outcome Comparative Study of Psychiatric Hospitals.* New York, Pergamon, 1967.

United States Department of Health, Education & Welfare: *Mental Retardation Source Book of the Department of HEW.* Washington, D.C., Office of MR Coordination.

Vander Kolk, Charles J.: Physiological measures as a means of assessing reactions to the disabled. *New Outlook for the Blind,* American Foundation for the Blind, March 1976.

Von Hagen, Victor W.: *World of the Maya.* New York, NAL, 1960.

INDEX

M

N

O

S

X

Z